CROSS STITCH
BORDERS and MOTIFS

Also by Jana Hauschild Lindberg
and published by Cassell

Scandinavian Cross Stitch Designs (1996)

Cross Stitch Animals (1994)

Flowers in Cross Stitch (1992)

Making Gifts in Counted Cross Stitch (1990)

CROSS STITCH
BORDERS
and MOTIFS

JANA HAUSCHILD LINDBERG

WARD LOCK

A WARD LOCK BOOK

First published in the UK 1998
by Ward Lock
Wellington House
125 Strand
LONDON
WC2R 0BB

A Cassell Imprint

A British Library Cataloguing in Publication Data block for this
book may be obtained from the British Library.

ISBN 0-7063-7679-X

Edited by Wendy Hobson
Designed and typeset by Ian Hunt and Linda Henley
Charts by Design Partner, Copenhagen
Printed by South China Printing Co. Ltd,
Hong Kong/China

CONTENTS

INTRODUCTION

Whenever you are researching and writing a book, you always collect a number of ideas which, for one reason or another, don't quite fall within the chosen topic and therefore have to be discarded. But since no designer ever completely discards a good idea, I have collected all those projects together and found that they create a book of their own: this book on cross stitch borders and motifs.

The essence of the book is to show you a range of border and motif designs and projects which you can use to create beautiful embroideries for your home. In addition to this, learning how the shapes and designs interact will lead you on to being more adventurous in creating your own unique cross-stitch designs.

The border and motif designs included in the book come from a range of sources: flowers and fruit, birds and animals, people and homes, abstract shapes and patterns. Examining the ideas presented and investigating your own designs, you will soon see the vast potential open to you.

The complete alphabets of simple and decorative letters act as a base for those who would like to personalize gifts or create their own samplers, while the zodiac sun-signs can be used for gift cards, pictures and many other projects.

Each chapter is organized so that the source material appears first, followed by simple, then progressively more complex groups of projects, each with full information on how to prepare, stitch and finish the item. It is a good idea to read through the introductory material first so that you first understand the principles on which you are working.

The wonderful thing about a collection such as this is that the beginner can find complete projects to follow, enabling them to create beautiful pictures, greetings cards, table linen or other items as gifts or for the home; while the experienced cross stitcher can select different motifs and mix and match them with complementary borders or elements of other designs, creating unique and original work. Needless to say, the book also caters for every stage in between.

So look through the information on the techniques and principles of this delightful craft, then launch into some of the fascinating projects which you can create for your home.

COUNTED CROSS STITCH
TECHNIQUES AND PROJECTS

Counted cross stitch is one of the simplest forms of embroidery. It consists of a series of cross stitches embroidered on an evenweave fabric over the intersection of the horizontal and vertical threads. The stitches are worked following a chart. Each cross stitch is indicated by a symbol on the chart; the different symbols represent different colours, as you can see in the sample chart of the border below. You can work the design as directed in the colour key, or make up your own original colour scheme.

The size of a cross stitch design is determined by the type of fabric on which it is embroidered. Although finished sizes are given for the designs in this book, it is easy to calculate a different finished size by using the following formula:

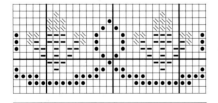

●	869	brown
▬	907	light green
◩	3607	light cyclamen

Figure 1: Symbols indicate different colours

Finished size = number of stitches divided by thread count of fabric.

For example, you have selected a design that is 42 stitches wide and 98 stitches long and would like to work on a cloth that has $5\frac{1}{2}$ threads per cm ($13\frac{1}{2}$ threads per in). The finished size can be determined by dividing the number of stitches (42 or 98) by the numbers of threads ($5\frac{1}{2}$ or $13\frac{1}{2}$) which gives you a design that is 7.5 x 18cm (3 x 7in).

If you feel this size is too large, switch to a linen cloth which has 10 threads per cm (25 threads per in). The size in that case would be approximately 4 x 10cm ($1\frac{1}{2}$ x 4in). Use this formula to decide quickly which thread count of fabric to use.

MATERIALS
Fabric
You can use any evenweave fabric made from cotton, linen, wool or synthetic blends. The fabrics used in this book include linen and Aida. Linen measures are given in threads, Aida measures in stitches.

Counted-thread fabrics specially woven for cross stitch, such as Aida, Hardanger, Ainring and Binca, are available in most needlecraft shops. They have clearly defined holes for stitching. Aida fabric is the most widely available. It is cotton and can

be bought in a range of sizes, the most common being: $4\frac{1}{2}$, $5\frac{1}{2}$ and 7 stitches per cm (11, $13\frac{1}{2}$ and 18 stitches per in). Hardanger cloth is available in linen or cotton.

If you would like to embroider on an unusual-coloured fabric, or one with less clearly defined stitching holes, try using linen, which is available in most fabric shops. Check that the weave of your material has an equal number of threads vertically and horizontally. If the difference is too big, the embroidery will be deformed. When using linen, you will have to take into account the inevitable slubs and inconsistencies that occur naturally in the weave; this is why it is to best work counted cross stitch over two or more threads on linen fabric (see figure 7), as this gives you the chance to adjust an area of stitching if necessary. Twenty-eight or 30-count linen will give much the same effect as working on 14-count Aida cloth. All the designs on linen in the book are worked over two stitches.

Counted cross stitch designs in which the background is stitched may also be worked on needlepoint canvas. In this case, tapestry or crewel wools may be used instead of embroidery thread (floss) to create hard-wearing soft furnishing items.

When choosing a fabric, think about what it will be used for and whether it needs to be washed. For items such as tablecloths, it is worth using a good-quality fabric.

You are best to work either in metric or imperial measures otherwise it can be confusing. Remember:

For linen:
6 threads per cm = 15 threads per in
8 threads per cm = 20 threads per in
10 threads per cm = 25 threads per in

For Aida:
4½ stitches per cm = 11 threads per in
5½ stitches per cm = 13½ threads per in
7 stitches per cm = 18 stitches per in

Threads and Yarns
Six-strand cotton embroidery thread (floss) is ideal for counted cross stitch because the thread can be separated into the exact number of strands that provide the correct amount of coverage. Use thread or yarn that is the same thickness as the threads of the fabric you are to embroider. For flatter designs, separate the strands of thread and work with two strands in your needle. If you wish to create a more textured effect, use more strands. You can also use silk or metallic threads, Danish mohair, pearl cotton, even crewel wool, depending on the thread count of your fabric. To add some sparkle to a design, mix one strand of metallic thread with two strands of embroidery thread (floss).

Throughout this book I have referred to DMC six-strand embroidery thread (floss). A conversion chart on page 20 shows at a glance where you can make substitutions with Anchor threads.

EQUIPMENT
Needles
Use a small, blunt tapestry needle, size number 24 or 26, to avoid splitting the fabric threads. A crewel or chenille needle is useful for working with waste canvas (see page 10).

Hoop
Work with a small, round embroidery hoop, which consists of an inner ring and an adjustable outer ring that tightens by turning a screw. Always remove your work from the ring at the end of stitching so that it does not pull out of shape, and keep the work in a clean pillow case.

Scissors
You must have a pair of small, sharp embroidery scissors for cutting threads and a pair of sharp fabric shears for cutting out fabric.

TECHNIQUES
Full instructions on specific projects are given at the end of this chapter. This section gives you the basic techniques of cross stitch.

Choose your fabric and work out the correct size required for the project (see page 8), then add about 2.5cm (1in) around the edges and cut out the fabric. Count the size of the chosen motif on the fabric to double-check that it takes the desired amount of space. If you are working a circular design, draw a circle by placing a pin on your tape measure 1cm (½in) longer than the radius of the circle, and drawing round the circle through the hole in the end of the tape. Overcast the edges to prevent unravelling.

Find the centre of the fabric by folding it in half crossways and lengthways; mark the centre point with a small stitch. Then find the centre point of your design, which is usually indicated on the chart by arrows. Do not begin your design in the centre; instead, count the number of squares on the chart from the centre point to the top, then count the same number of squares to the top of your fabric and work your first stitch there.

Place the fabric in the embroidery hoop so that it is taut. Adjust the tension as you work so that the fabric is always firmly held.

Work the design in horizontal rows of colour from left to right.

Begin stitching by leaving a length of waste thread at the back of the work, securing it with your first few stitches, as shown in figure 2.

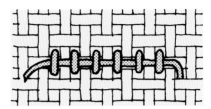

Figure 2: Secure your thread at the back of the work

Insert your needle into the holes of the fabric, working one slanted stitch over the intersection of two threads from lower right to upper left, as shown in figure 3.

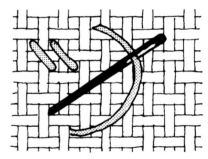

Figure 3: Work the first diagonal from lower right to upper left

Continue working the required number of slanting stitches across the row, following the symbols on the chart. Then work back across the row, making slanting stitches from lower left to upper right to finish each cross stitch, as shown in figure 4.

Figure 4: Work back across the stitches to complete the crosses

In Denmark and America, stitches are worked from lower left to upper right, then crossed from lower right to upper left. It makes no difference which way you stitch, as long as all the stitches are crossed in the same direction.

When you are working a vertical row of stitches, cross each stitch in turn, as shown in figure 5.

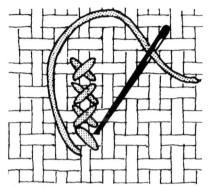

Figure 5: Cross each stitch in turn on vertical rows

To end a line of stitching, finish your last stitch and keep the needle and thread on the wrong side of the work. Wiggle the point of the needle beneath a few threads on the wrong side and pull the thread through as shown in figure 6. Clip off the excess thread so that the ends will not show through on the right side of the work.

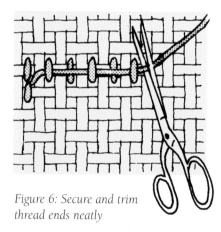

Figure 6: Secure and trim thread ends neatly

If you are working on linen, or if you wish to make larger stitches, work over two sets of threads in each direction, as shown in figure 7.

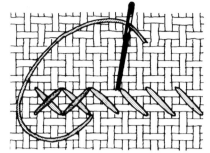

Figure 7: Cross stitches worked over two fabric threads

Back Stitch

Back stitch is commonly used in conjunction with counted cross stitch to outline, delineate features or emphasize a portion of the design. Work the back stitches from one hole to the next in a horizontal, vertical or diagonal direction, as show in figure 8.

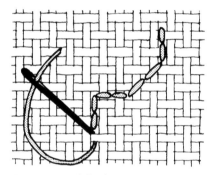

Figure 8: Work back stitch over one thread in any direction

Working with Waste Canvas

Counted cross stitch can be worked on non-evenweave fabrics by using a non-interlock waste canvas. This is particularly suitable for knitted or finer fabrics. Select a canvas with a stitch count of the desired size. Cut the canvas 2.5cm (1in) larger than the finished size of your design. Tack (baste) the canvas to your chosen fabric in the area you wish to embroider. Using a crewel or chenille needle, work the design over the canvas. As you work, pass the needle straight up and down through the fabric and canvas; take great care not to catch the canvas threads in your embroidery. When the embroidery is finished, remove

the tacking and dampen the canvas thoroughly using a warm, wet towel. Gently pull out the canvas threads one by one, using tweezers if necessary.

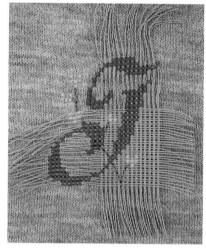

Using waste canvas

Finishing your Work

When you have finished your embroidery, remove it from the hoop and press it lightly with a damp cloth. Make up as indicated in the individual projects.

Mitring Corners

To make sure your hem is flat on a rectangular project, mitred corners are essential. Fold over and press the hem on all sides, then open out. Fold the corner across the diagonal so that the fold crosses the hem line. Trim to 5mm/¼in. Fold back the hem over the top and slip stitch in place. Press lightly.

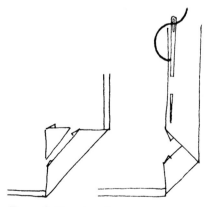

Figure 9: How to mitre corners

CREATING YOUR OWN DESIGNS

Beginners will be happy working through the range of designs and projects included in this book, but once you gain more experience, you will begin to see opportunities for creating your own unique designs. The first stage in that process is to mix and match motifs, borders and patterns from within the book, or to extract elements of the designs to use in a different way. After that, you may want to start from scratch and look for other sources of design ideas. Whichever route you are taking, the process is very much the same.

The first thing to think about is the scale of your project and what type of design would be suitable. Are you going to embroider a handkerchief for a gift, a footstool or a large tablecloth? For the first, you need to think about a delicate motif, the second may demand an overall design, perhaps in a thicker tapestry wool, and the third will look best with a broad border design or large central motif.

Next, consider subjects and colours. If the handkerchief is a gift, what are the recipient's favourite colours? Does the footstool have to

Bluebell Cushion

match a particular room decor? If you have decided on a cornflour design for your tablecloth, then clearly you will be working in blues and greens.

If you are thinking about creating a motif, then it must have a coherent shape. A circle or an oval is a good beginning, but it is the balance of the shape that is most important. Don't leave a long trail of ivy from one side of a motif without something to counterbalance it. Select elements from existing designs and think about how they might work together. A butterfly from one design may look excellent matched with a flower from another, for example.

An all-over design is put together by repeating a single motif or a series of motifs. Tiny motifs arranged close together will have a different effect to larger motifs more widely spaced, especially if you choose two or three designs to repeat rather than one. Wallpaper books are a good source of ideas and effects. Look at any of the designs in the book and lift out tiny parts – perhaps a flower head, a fruit or a pattern shape – and think about whether they will work independently. The more elements you add, the more complex the design will become – that is up to you.

Footstool

Notice Board with Flowers

If it is a border design you are planning, then the shape of the finished object will give you your basic outline, and the object itself will dictate how wide the border should be. A narrow border looks best with a very small repeat pattern, while a wide border will need a larger pattern motif.

Experienced cross stitchers will find that they begin to see potential designs everywhere: the pattern in a bouquet of flowers, an unusual leaf shape, an attractive fabric or a row of books on a shelf. Keeping a little notebook where you scribble down design ideas or stick in pieces of fabric, pressed flowers, postcards, photographs or anything else that might inspire you, is a good idea. Then when you have the time and inclination, you need never be searching for ideas while staring at that blank piece of graph paper.

New Designs from Old

Now that you have the basic ideas, look through the patterns and begin to select sections from motifs or borders that suit your style. Copy the outlines roughly on to small pieces of tracing paper so that you can move them around on a plain sheet of paper and see how they relate to one another. This will reveal that some don't work together

at all, while others are naturally complementary. Think about the shapes between the cross stitch elements themselves as well as the embroidered shapes. Motifs will not look as attractive if they are too close together.

If you are using a border design to make a frame, you will need to work out the corner of the pattern by drawing it on squared paper. Count along the design from the centre to the position on the chart where the corner will fall. Place a mirror diagonally across the corner of the chart and copy the pattern on the paper. Always start stitching in the centre of a border so that the sides are even. The illustration shows how to use the mirror to create a corner pattern.

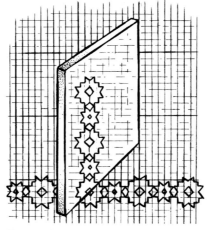

Figure 10: Using a mirror to create a corner pattern.

Once you have a good plan of the elements you want to use, copy the design elements in coloured pencils, again on small pieces of tracing paper, then move them around and eventually stick them down on to graph paper to create your design. Alterna-

Wild Rose Border

Initial circled by flowers

tively, use water-soluble felt pens on a film pad with interleaved grid sheets to work out designs. If you wish, copy it neatly on to graph paper, remembering to make a key of the colours as you go. Especially if you have a number of similar colours, it is a good idea to number your coloured pencils on the pencils themselves and on the key as it makes it easier to match up with your threads.

Choose your threads to match as closely as possible to the colours you have drawn. With the vast range of colours available, you should find suitable matches. However, in looking at thread colours – which are obviously different from the coloured pencils – you may find that new ideas for colour combinations inspire you and you can continue to make changes until you are ready to stitch.

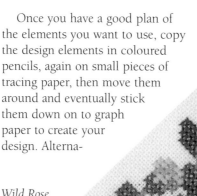

Traditional Sampler

Making a Sampler

All Victorian young ladies had to work their own samplers, and they do make beautiful decorations for the home, and heirlooms to pass on to your children. The essence of a sampler is that you combine images relevant to you personally, so think carefully about what you want to include and spend some time working out the design. Most samplers contain an upper and lower case alphabet and sometimes the sequence of numbers. You can include your favourite flowers, initials, representations of your home, your family and pets. Think about using symbolic motifs: a flower and trowel for an interest in gardening, some sewing threads, cooking utensils, a football or club badge and so on. Other samplers will give you ideas, but don't be afraid to include anything you particularly like. Embroider the date of completion, press and frame the sampler (see page 16) so that it will keep for many years.

SMALL PROJECTS

Instructions for making up the simpler projects in this book are given here. More complicated making-up instructions may be given under the project itself. You can use any designs – from those given in the book or your own individual creations – to make up any of the following items.

Bookmark

Cut a piece of evenweave fabric about 10 x 30cm (4 x 12in) and overcast the raw edges. Embroider a small motif or border design on the fabric, leaving room around the edges to make up the bookmark. Trim away any frayed edges and the overcast edges at the top and bottom. Gently press the finished embroidery. Fold the long edges 6mm (¼in) to the wrong side, then fold over again 2cm (¾in) and slip stitch neatly in place. Carefully draw threads away from the top and bottom edges to make fringes about 1cm (½in) deep at each end.

Framed Picture, Greeting Cards and a Sachet

Bookmarks

You can also buy ready-made strips of evenweave fabric which are designed for stitching bookmarks and borders.

Gift Tag, Place Card or Name Label

Calculate the finished size of your design using the formula on page 8. Cut a piece of evenweave fabric about 2.5cm (1in) larger than the finished size and overcast the raw edges. Embroider a small motif on the fabric and gently press the finished embroidery. Cut away excess fabric, leaving about 1cm (½in) all round the edge of the design. Carefully pull away threads from the cut edges, creating a 6mm

(¼in) fringe. Press lightly. Glue the wrong side of the design to a piece of card.

Greetings Cards

Choose a design that will fit within the window of a blank greetings card, which you can buy from handicraft shops. If you wish to make your own, cut a piece of good-quality card about 15 x 30cm (6 x 12in), then divide the length into thirds, making the right-hand piece 1mm wider than the other two. Cut a circle or rectangle out of the central section, leaving about a 2cm (¾in) border. Score the fold lines lightly, then fold the outer sections over the centre. You can adapt this principle to make any size of card, but use a thick card for larger items. Cut a piece of evenweave fabric about 2cm (½in) larger than the finished size of the card aperture all round and overcast the raw edges. Embroider a motif in the centre of the fabric and gently press the finished embroidery. Trim off the overcast edges. Open out the card with the largest section on the right and glue all over the border in the centre section or use double-sided tape. Stick the embroidery face down on the card, then fold over and stick down the smaller of the outer sections to make the card.

Pin Cushion or Sachet

Calculate the finished size of your design using the formula on page 8. Cut a piece of evenweave fabric about 2.5cm (1in) larger than the finished size and overcast the raw edges. Embroider a small motif on the centre of the fabric and press lightly. Cut away excess fabric to the desired size, including a 6mm (¼in) seam allowance. Cut a matching piece of fabric for the back. With right sides facing, stitch round 6mm (¼in) from the edge, leaving an opening on the centre of one side for turning. Trim the corners at a diagonal, then turn to the right side and press lightly. Stuff with polyester filling or pot pourri until plump. Fold in the raw edges at the opening and slip stitch the opening closed.

Matchbox or Box Cover

Cut a piece of evenweave fabric about 2.5cm (1in) larger than the desired finished size and overcast the raw edges. Embroider a small motif on the fabric and gently press the finished embroidery. Cut away excess fabric to the exact size of the matchbox you wish to cover. Glue the wrong side of the design to the top of the matchbox, making sure the raw edges are securely glued so that they do not unravel.

Poinsettia Border

Use the same technique for covering a small box to store a piece of jewellery.

Pocket

Use a commercial patch pocket pattern, or make a pattern in greaseproof (waxed) paper based on a pocket on an item you already have. Cut one pocket from evenweave fabric, including a 6mm (¼in) seam allowance. Embroider a small motif in the centre of the fabric and gently press the finished embroidery. Cut a matching piece of fabric for the lining. With right sides facing, stitch round 6mm (¼in) from the edge, leaving an opening

on the centre of one side for turning. Trim the corners at a diagonal, then turn to the right side. Fold in the raw edges at the opening, slip stitch the opening closed, then press lightly. Top stitch the edges of the pocket, if desired, then sew to the front of a blouse or skirt with small slip stitches.

Tie or Collar

Select a small design and cut a piece of waste canvas 2.5cm (1in) larger than the finished design. Centre the waste canvas on a tie or collar and tack (baste) in place. Work the design over the canvas, then remove the canvas threads (see page 10). Gently press the finished embroidery.

Handkerchief

Select a small design and cut a piece of waste canvas 2.5cm (1in) larger than the finished design. Position the waste canvas in the corner of a handkerchief and tack (baste) in place. Work the design over the canvas, then remove the canvas threads (see page 10). Gently press the finished embroidery. Sew a strip of lace around the edge of the handkerchief, if you wish.

Handkerchief and Embroidered Jumper

T-shirt or Jumper

Select a medium or large design and cut a piece of waste canvas 2.5cm (1in) larger than the finished design. Centre the waste canvas on the front of a T-shirt and tack (baste) in place. Work the design over the canvas, then remove the canvas threads (see page 10). Gently press the finished embroidery.

Baby's Bib

Cut a piece of evenweave fabric about 6mm (¼in) larger than the desired finished size and overcast the raw edges. Find the centre of the bib at the neckline. Begin working a small design about 2.5cm (1in) below the raw neck edge or in the exact centre of the bib front, then gently press the finished embroidery. Trim away the overcast edges, then finish the raw edges of the bib with bias binding, leaving a length of binding at the back for tying.

Christmas Ornaments

Calculate the finished size of your design using the formula on page 8. Cut a piece of evenweave fabric about 6mm (¼in) larger than the finished size and overcast the raw edges. Embroider a small motif in the centre of the fabric and gently press the finished embroidery. Cut away excess fabric to the desired size, including a 6mm (¼in) seam allowance, making the decoration into an attractive shape. Cut a matching piece of fabric for the back. With right sides facing, stitch round 6mm (¼in) from the edge, leaving an opening on the centre of one side for turning. Trim any corners at a diagonal and clip any curves, then turn to the right side and press lightly. Stuff with polyester filling until plump. Fold in the raw edges at the opening and slip stitch the opening closed.

Unframed Cross Stitch Picture or Notice Board

Calculate the finished size of your design using the formula on page 8. Cut a piece of evenweave fabric about 5cm (2in) larger than the size of your picture and overcast the raw edges. Work the picture in the centre of the fabric, then gently press the finished embroidery. Cut a piece of card to the same size as the finished picture. Place the embroidery face-down on a flat surface and centre the card on top. Spread glue or stick double-sided tape around the edges of the card, then fold over the corners at a diagonal. Spread more glue on the fabric and press the fabric on to the glue all round the picture. To neaten the back, cut a piece of paper slightly smaller than the picture and glue to the back.

For a larger piece, it is better to fix the embroidery to the board by stitching threads vertically and horizontally across the back of the back of the board to hold the embroidery firmly in place, rather than using glue or tape.

Framed Picture

You can buy all kinds of embroidery frames from handicraft shops and if you have a special piece of work which you want to protect from dust, then a glass-fronted frame is essential. Proceed in the same way as for the unframed picture, then trim to size and fit into the frame according to the manufacturer's instructions. For the most special pieces, you can contact a professional picture framer who deals with fabric pieces.

Notice Board with Fish

DECORATING THE HOME

Wall Hanging

Calculate the finished size of your design using the formula on page 8. Cut a piece of evenweave fabric 5cm (2in) larger all round than the calculated size and overcast the raw edges. Work the design from the top in the centre of the fabric, then gently press the finished embroidery. Measure 3.5cm (1⅜in) from the outer edge of the embroidery at the sides and bottom and trim away the excess fabric. Trim away only the overcast edges at the top. Fold the fabric at the side and bottom edges 6mm (¼in) to the wrong side, then fold over again 1cm (½in), mitring the corners (see page 10). Tack (baste) and slip stitch neatly in place. For the casing at the top edge, press the raw edge 6mm (¼in) to the wrong side, then fold down 2cm (¾in) and slip stitch firmly in place. Gently press the finished wall hanging. Insert a brass or wooden rod through the casing.

Table Runner

Calculate the finished size of your design using the formula on page 8. Cut a piece of evenweave fabric 5cm (2in) larger all round than the finished size and overcast the raw edges. Decide where you wish to place the design, then embroider your chosen design, including a border all round the table runner, if desired. Gently press the finished embroidery. Trim away excess fabric, leaving 2cm (¾in) for hemming. Fold the edges 6mm (¼in) to the wrong side, then fold over again 1cm (½in), mitring the corners (see page 10). Tack (baste) and slip stitch neatly in place. Press lightly.

Curtain Tie-backs or Lampshade Trim

Calculate the finished size of your design using the formula on page 8. Cut a piece of evenweave fabric 2.5cm (1in) longer than required

Christmas Table Runner

and deep enough for the design plus 1cm (½in), and overcast the raw edges. Embroider a design along the centre of the fabric, then gently press the finished embroidery. Cut matching pieces of interfacing and lining. Tack (baste) the interfacing to the wrong side of the embroidery. With right sides facing, stitch the lining to the embroidery 1cm (½in) from the top and bottom edges, then turn to the right side and press lightly. For a tie-back, fold in the raw edges at the ends and slip stitch closed. Apply Velcro touch-and-close fastener to secure the ends together. For a lampshade trim, fold the raw edges at one end to the inside. Slip stitch or glue the embroidery around the bottom edge of the lampshade, slipping the raw edges inside the folded edge. Slip stitch to secure.

Curtain

Measure your window and cut a piece of evenweave fabric. The depth should be the depth of the window plus a 1cm (½in) hem at

Favourite Flowers Wall Hanging

the top and a 5cm (2in) hem at the bottom. The width should be the width of the window multiplied by about 1¼; the curtain should not be very full. Hem the bottom edge of the curtain and overcast the raw edges. Begin working a border design in the centre of the fabric

Deer and Woodland Cushion

just above the hem and working outward to each side edge. When finished, hem the side edges of the curtain. Attach rufflette tape at the top of the curtain, turning in the raw edges, or attach loops of fabric to make a café-style curtain. Gently press the finished curtain.

Cushion

Calculate the finished size of your design using the formula on page 8. Cut a piece of evenweave fabric 5cm (2in) larger all round than the finished size and overcast the raw edges. Work the design in the centre of the fabric, then gently press the finished embroidery. Cut away excess fabric to the desired size, including a 6mm (¼in) seam allowance. Cut a matching piece of fabric for the back. With right sides facing, stitch round 6mm (¼in) from the edge, leaving an opening

on the centre of one side for turning. Trim the corners at a diagonal, then turn to the right side and press lightly. Stuff with polyester filling until plump. Fold in the raw edges at the opening and slip stitch the opening closed, or fit a zip (zipper).

Bath Towel Edging

Calculate the finished size of your design using the formula on page 8. Cut a piece of evenweave fabric 2.5cm (1in) longer than the width of your towel, and 2.5cm (1in) wider than the design. Overcast the raw edges. Work a border design from the centre along the length of the fabric, then gently press the finished embroidery. Trim off the overcast edges. Fold the raw edges of the embroidery 6mm (¼in) to the wrong side and tack, then slip stitch securely to the towel.

FOR THE KITCHEN AND DINING ROOM

Pot-holder

Cut a piece of evenweave fabric about 18–23cm (7–9in) square and overcast the raw edges. Select a design that will fit nicely on the fabric and embroider the design on the centre of the fabric, then gently press the finished embroidery. Trim off the overcast edges. Cut a matching piece of fabric for the back and two or three layers of cotton or wool padding (do not use polyester). Sandwich the padding between the embroidery and the back; tack (baste) the edges together. Finish the edges with bias binding, allowing excess binding at one corner to make a hanging loop. Remove the tacking (basting) stitches.

Egg Cosy

Cut two pieces of evenweave fabric 2.5cm (1in) larger all round than the finished size of the egg cosy and overcast the raw edges. Decide where you want to place the design, then embroider it on both pieces of fabric. Gently press the finished embroidery. Cut two matching pieces of iron-on interfacing and iron one to the back of each piece of fabric. Cut away any excess fabric. With right sides facing, machine stitch the two pieces together, leaving the lower edge open. Clip any curves, then turn to the right side. Turn in the lower edges and slip stitch together, then press lightly. Stitch a cord in place around the seam.

Shelf Border

Cut a piece of evenweave fabric 2.5cm (1in) longer than your shelf and wide enough for the design plus 1cm (½in). Overcast the raw edges. Embroider a border design along the centre of the fabric, then gently press the finished embroidery. Trim off the overcast edges. Cut a matching piece of interfacing and

Blackberry Towel Edging

Christmas Table Linen

tack (baste) to the wrong side of the embroidery. Fold the raw edges of the embroidery 6mm (¼in) to the wrong side and secure to the interfacing with small slip stitches, then press lightly. Pin, glue or Velcro the border to the front of your cupboard shelf.

Rectangular Table Linen

Use this technique to make a tablecloth, traycloth, centrepiece, place mat, plate liner or doily. Cut a piece of evenweave fabric 2.5cm (1in) larger all round than the finished size of the item and overcast the raw edges. Decide where you wish to place the design. Embroider the design, adding a border all round the motif, if desired. Gently press the finished embroidery. Cut away excess fabric, leaving 2cm (¾in) for a hem. Fold the fabric 6mm (¼in) to the wrong side, then fold over again 2cm (¾in), mitring the corners (see page 10), tack (baste), then slip stitch neatly in place. Trim the edge with lace, if you wish. Press lightly.

Round Tablecloth or Centrepiece

Calculate the finished size of your design using the formula on page 8. Cut a piece of evenweave fabric 3.5cm (1⅜in) larger than the finished size all round and overcast the raw edges. Find the exact centre of the fabric and the design and mark the fabric with a tacking (basting) thread. Count from the centre of the graph and the fabric to start the design. Work the graph, which gives one-quarter of the design, then turn the fabric clockwise and work the next quarter. Continue turning and repeating until the pattern is finished. Gently press the finished embroidery. Measure 3cm (1¼in) from the outer edge of the embroidery and trim off the excess fabric. Fold the fabric 6mm (¼in) to the wrong side, then fold over 6mm (¼in) again, tack (baste), then slip stitch neatly in place. Press lightly.

Round Doily, Traycloth, Plate Liner or Place Mat

Follow the instructions for making the round tablecloth, but for smaller items, cut your evenweave fabric 2.5cm (1in) larger than the finished size all round. Finish the edges with bias binding, if you wish, rather than a hem.

Jar Cover

Cut out a circle of evenweave fabric 5cm (2in) larger than the lid. Oversew or zigzag the edge, then fold back about 1cm (½in) to the wrong side. Tack (baste) the lace to the hem, then machine stitch in place. Alternatively, finish the edge with bias binding. Tie on to the jar or bottle with a matching ribbon.

Napkin Ring

Cut a piece of evenweave fabric about 9 x 15cm (3½ x 6in) and overcast the raw edges. Embroider a 3cm (1¼in) high motif or border design along the centre of the fabric, then gently press the finished embroidery. Trim away the overcast edges. Fold the fabric in half lengthways with right sides facing, and stitch a seam 6mm (¼in) from the long edge. Position the embroidery in the centre of the strip and press the seam open flat, then turn to the right side and press lightly. Fold the raw edges at one end to the inside. Shape the napkin ring into a circle, slipping the raw edges inside the folded edge. Slip stitch to secure.

SIX-STRAND EMBROIDERY CONVERSION CHART

DMC	ANCHOR	DMC	ANCHOR	DMC	ANCHOR	DMC	ANCHOR	DMC	ANCHOR	DMC	ANCHOR	DMC	ANCHOR	DMC	ANCHOR
white	2	402	1047	601	(63)*	744	301	833	(907)*	945	881	3052	859*	3761	928*
ecru	387	407	914	602	57	745	300	834	874	946	332*	3053	858*	3765	169*
208	111	413	401	603	62*	746	275	838	380	947	330	3064	883	3766	167*
209	109	414	235	604	55	747	158	839	(360)*	948	1011	3072	(847)	3768	779
210	108	415	398	605	(50)*	754	1012	840	379	950	4146	3078	292	3770	1009
211	342	420	374	606	335	758	9575*	841	378	951	1010	3325	129	3772	1007
221	897*	422	943*	608	332*	760	1022	842	376	954	203	3326	36	3773	1008
223	895	433	371	610	889	761	1021	844	1041*	955	206*	3328	1024	3774	778
224	893	434	310*	611	898	762	234	869	944	956	54	3340	329	3776	1048
225	1026	435	1046	612	832	772	259	890	(683)*	957	50*	3341	328	3777	1015
300	352	436	1045	613	831	775	128	891	35*	958	187*	3345	268*	3778	1013
301	1049*	437	362	632	936	776	24	892	28	959	186*	3346	267*	3779	868
304	1006	444	290	640	(903)*	778	968	893	41	961	76*	3347	266*	3781	1050
307	289	445	288	642	392	780	(310)*	894	26	962	75*	3348	264	3782	388
309	42	451	233	644	830	781	309	895	1044	963	73	3350	65	3787	(393)*
310	403	452	232	645	273	782	308	898	360*	964	185	3354	74	3790	393*
311	148	453	231	646	8581*	783	307	899	52	966	(206)*	3362	263	3799	236
312	979	469	267*	647	1040	791	178	900	333	970	(316)*	3363	262	B5200	1
315	1019*	470	267*	648	900	792	941	902	897*	971	316*	3364	(260)	3801	35*
316	1017	471	266*	666	46	793	176	904	258	972	298	3371	382	3802	(1019)*
317	400	472	(253)	676	891	794	175	905	257	973	297	3607	87	3803	972
318	399	498	(1005)*	677	886	796	133	906	256*	975	355	3608	86	3804	63*
319	218	500	683*	680	901*	797	132	907	255	976	1001	3609	85	3805	63*
320	215	501	878	699	923*	798	131	909	(923)*	977	1002	3685	1028	3806	(62)*
321	9046	502	876*	700	228	799	136	910	230	986	246	3687	68	3807	122
322	978	503	875*	701	227	800	144	911	205	987	244	3688	66	3808	(170)
326	59	504	1042	702	226	801	359	912	209	988	243	3689	49	3809	(169)*
327	100	517	162*	703	238	806	(168)*	913	204	989	242	3705	35*	3810	(168)*
333	119	518	1039	704	(256)*	807	168*	915	1029	991	(189)	3706	33	3811	(928)*
334	977	519	1038	712	926	809	130	917	89	992	187*	3708	31	3812	188*
335	38	520	862*	718	88	813	161*	918	341	993	186*	3712	1023	3813	875*
336	150	522	860	720	326	814	45	919	340	995	410	3713	1020	3814	(187)*
340	118	523	859*	721	324	815	43	920	1004	996	433	3716	25	3815	877
341	117	524	858*	722	323*	816	1005*	921	(884)	3011	845*	3721	896	3816	876*
347	1025	535	(1041)*	725	305*	817	13*	922	1003	3012	844	3722	1027	3817	875*
349	13*	543	933	726	295*	818	23	924	851	3013	842	3726	1018	3818	923*
350	(11)	550	101	727	293	819	271	926	850	3021	905	3727	1016	3819	278
351	10	552	99	729	890	820	134	927	848	3022	8581*	3731	(76)	3820	306
352	9	553	98	730	845	822	390	928	274	3023	(899)	3733	75*	3821	(305)*
353	6	554	(96)	731	924	823	(152)*	930	1035	3024	397	3740	873	3822	(295)*
355	1014	561	212	732	281*	824	164	931	1034	3031	360*	3743	869	3823	386
356	5975*	562	210	733	280*	825	162*	932	1033	3032	903*	3746	1030	3824	(9575)*
367	217	563	208	734	279	826	161*	934	862*	3033	391	3747	120	3825	(323)*
368	214	564	206*	738	361	827	160	935	861	3041	871	3750	1036	3826	1049*
369	1043	580	(281)*	739	366	828	9159	936	846	3042	870	3752	1032	3827	363
370	855	581	280*	740	316*	829	906	937	268*	3045	888	3753	1031	3828	943*
371	854	597	(168)*	741	304	830	277*	938	381	3046	887	3755	140	3829	901*
372	853	598	(167)*	742	303	831	(277)*	939	152*	3047	852	3756	1037	3830	5975*
400	351	600	78	743	302	832	907*	943	188*	3051	681	3760	(169)*		

This conversion chart should only be used as a guide since it is not always possible to provide exact comparisons.
• Anchor shades in brackets indicate the nearest equivalent shade.
• an * indicates that the Anchor shade has been used more than once and additional care should be taken to avoid duplication within a design.
Reproduced by permission of Coats Craft UK

2

BORDERS

$\mathcal{B}$ order designs are useful for edging towels or table linen, making shelf borders or Christmas decorations, or creating a frame for a motif or a collection of motifs. Try linking together complementary border designs to create something quite different, like the seat-cover or footstool projects on pages 126–7 and 128.

The first projects in this chapter concentrate on giving you some individual border designs to mix and match with other motifs and designs. The latter part of the chapter details complete projects which you can undertake as they stand, or use as a source of even more ideas for original work.

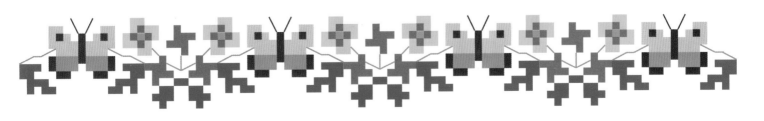

TRADITIONAL BORDERS

*T*his selection of borders shows you just the beginning of the range of borders you can use, selecting plain or fancy, straight or curved lines and using a simple border or incorporating a motif within a border frame.

Material
Aida with 5½ stitches per cm
  (13½ stitches per in)

Border widths
Gold and red 5mm (¼in)
Orange rectangles 1cm (½in)
Flowers and ribbon 2cm (¾in)
Green geometric 4cm (1½in)
Flower border 5cm (2in)

Thread
DMC embroidery thread. Use
  2 strands in the needle

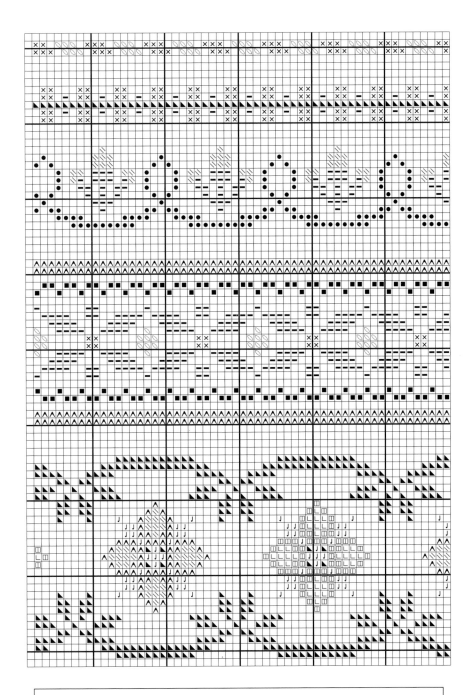

	869 brown		333 blue
	987 dark green		553 lilac
	907 light green		554 light lilac
	3819 light yellow-green		917 dark cyclamen
	351 light red		3607 light cyclamen
	742 gold		

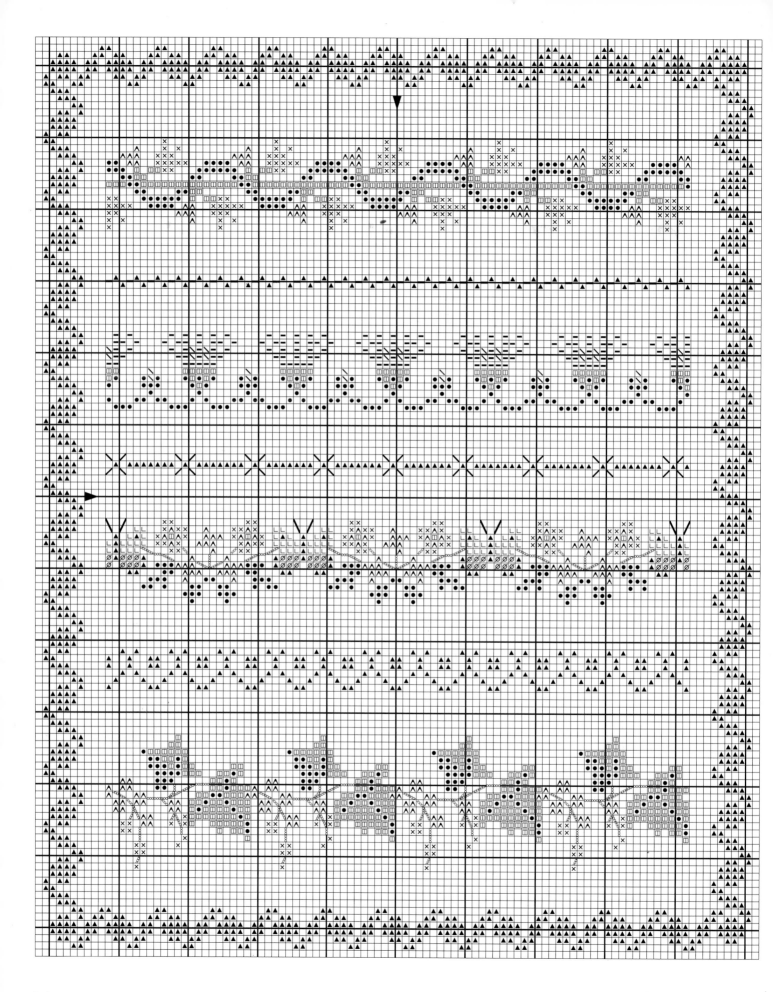

FLOWER BORDERS

Υou can create all sorts of border designs using simple flower motifs linked by a vine-effect stem. Remember to count the stitches for the border before you start so that you position it symmetrically and any corners are perfect.

Material
Aida with 5½ stitches per cm
   (11 stitches per in)

Border widths
Main border 1cm (½in)
Climbing plant 2.5cm (1in)
Brown border 6mm (¼in)
Thistle 2cm (¾in)
Star border 5mm (¼in)
Butterflies 2.5cm (1in)
Cups 1cm (½in)
Vine 4cm (1½in)

Thread
DMC embroidery thread. Use
   2 strands in the needle

●	987	green
⊡	581	yellow-green
▲	3787	brown
∅	340	blue
⌐	341	light blue
⊟	553	lilac
◥	917	cyclamen
◭	335	red
☒	899	light red
∘∘∘∘∘∘	581	yellow-green (back stitch)
—	3787	brown (back stitch)

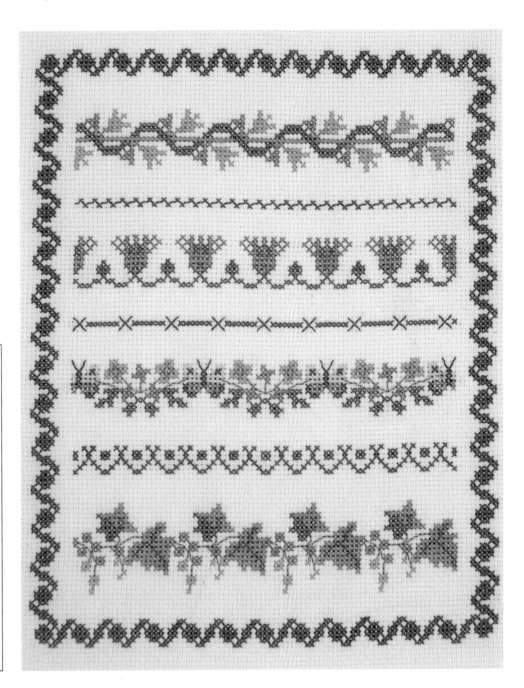

ANTIQUE BORDERS

Wider borders such as these often do not need a central motif, but look best ornamenting a tablecloth or other large item. Remember to count threads before you start; it is worth the extra time spent.

Material
Linen with 8 threads per cm
(20 threads per in)

Border widths
Blue flowers 4cm (1 ½in)
Green leaves 6cm (2 ½in)
Leaves and berries 8cm (3 ¼in)
Blue border 3cm (1 ¼in)

Thread
DMC embroidery
thread. Use 2 strands
in the needle

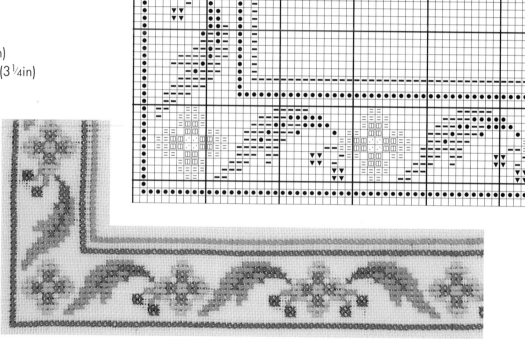

■	336	darkest blue
▼	825	dark blue
▥	826	medium blue
⊟	809	light blue
●	904	dark green
▬	703	medium green
⊠	907	light green
⊡	3819	yellow
◪	830	brown
⊙	3012	dull green

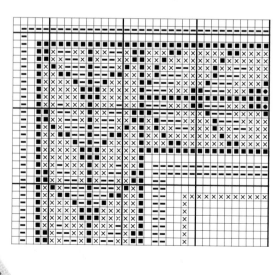

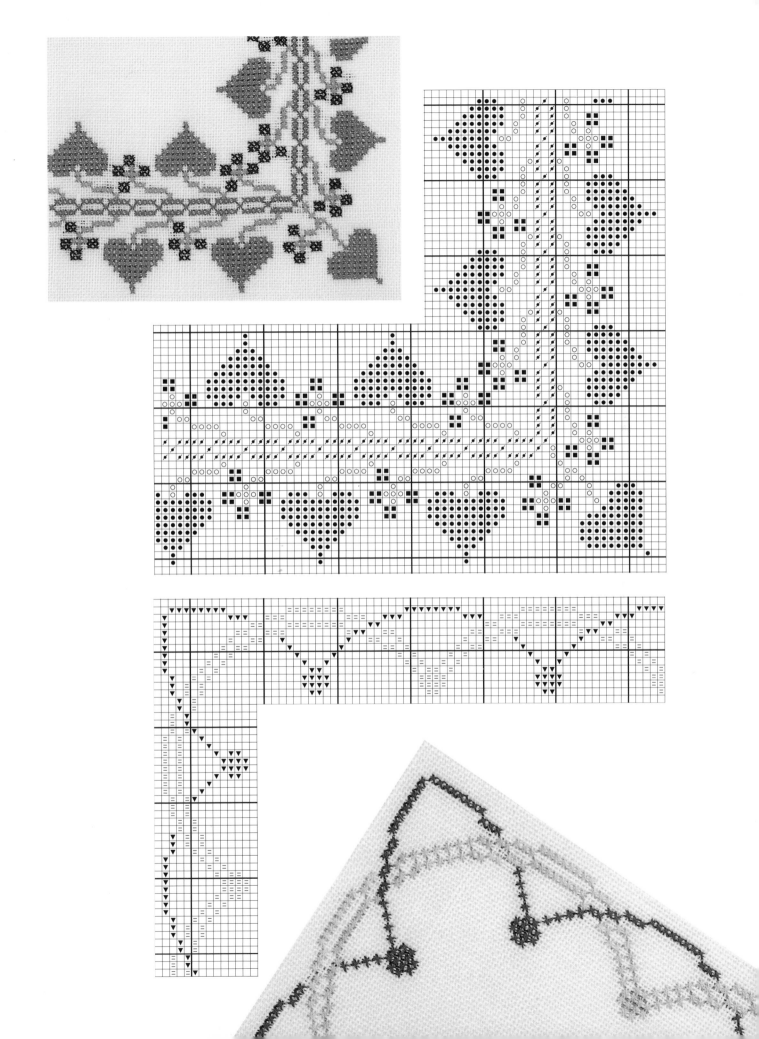

WILD ROSE AND CORNFLOWER BORDERS

*T*hese attractive borders would be perfect for a large cloth as they are strong enough to stand alone. Alternatively, you could combine them with a central motif or a tiny all-over rosebud or cornflower design in the centre of the fabric.

Material
Linen with 8 threads per cm
  (20 threads per in)

Border widths
Rose 6cm (2½in)
Cornflower 8cm (3¼in)

Thread
DMC embroidery thread. Use
  3 strands in the needle

Chart on page 30

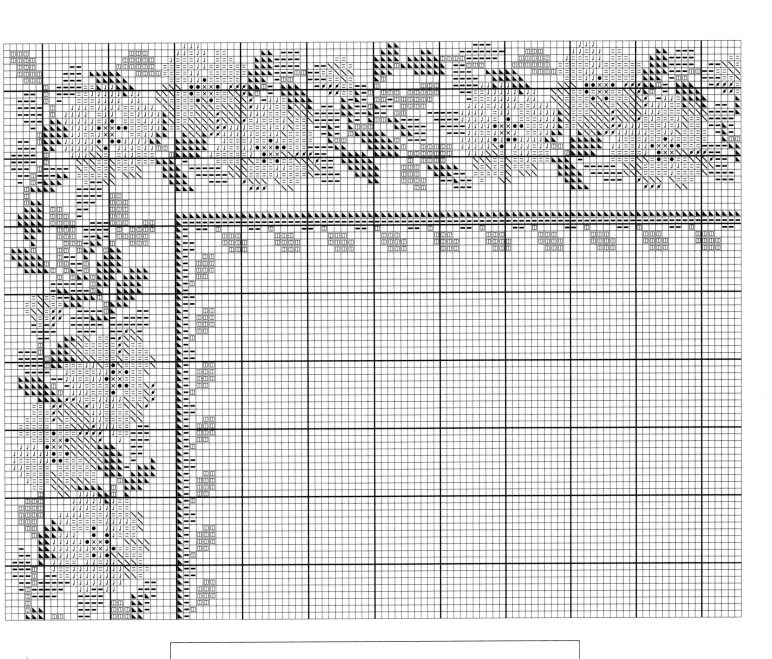

◣	3345	dark green		◿	3731	dark rose
▬	904	medium green		◥	3326	medium rose
▥	906	light green		⊟	3716	light rose
●	780	brown		ᴊ	3689	lightest rose
⊠	743	yellow				

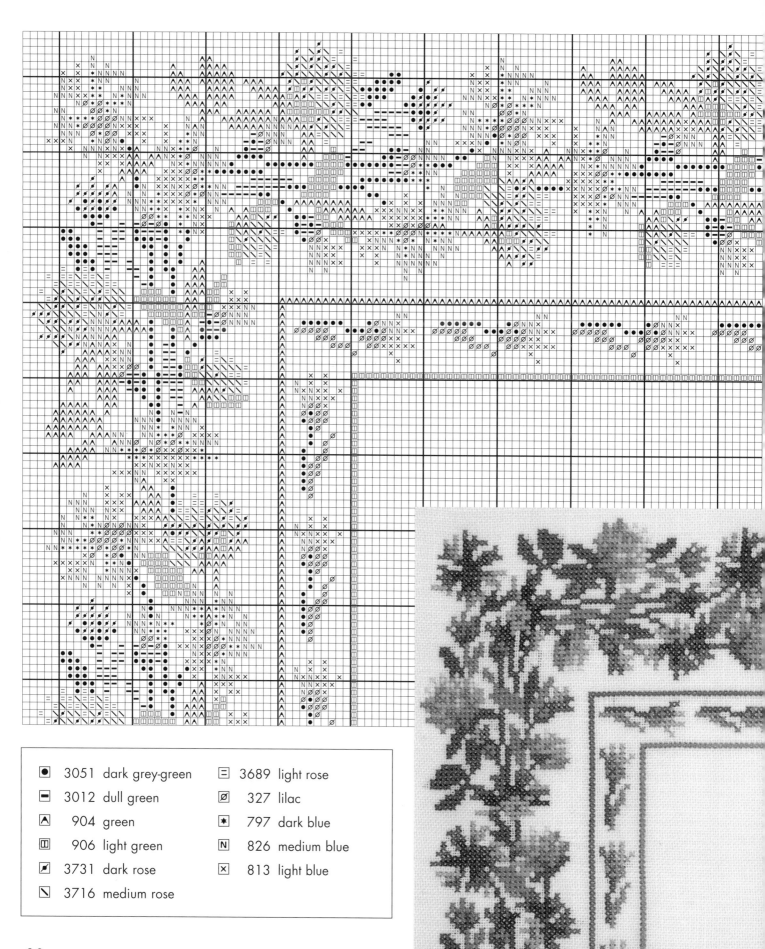

Symbol	Number	Colour
●	3051	dark grey-green
▬	3012	dull green
◭	904	green
▥	906	light green
◪	3731	dark rose
◥	3716	medium rose
═	3689	light rose
∅	327	lilac
✳	797	dark blue
N	826	medium blue
⊠	813	light blue

BORDER WITH DUCKS

*T*his would make an attractive border for a nursery item, or a collection of towels in the bathroom. Alternatively you could use one duck or several ducks as motifs on a jumper or child's pocket.

Material
Coloured evenweave with 10 thread per cm (25 threads per in)

Border width
5.5cm (2¼in)

Thread
DMC embroidery thread. Use 2 strands in the needle

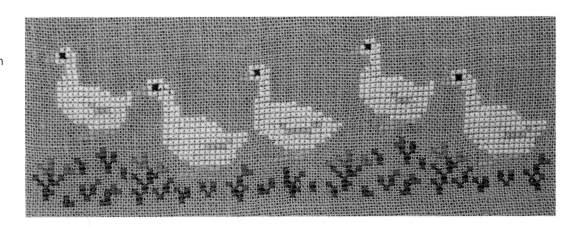

■ 3021 brown	J white	◪ 601 red
◮ 905 green	⊘ 741 orange	◩ 3607 rose
⊠ 3752 light blue		

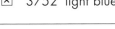

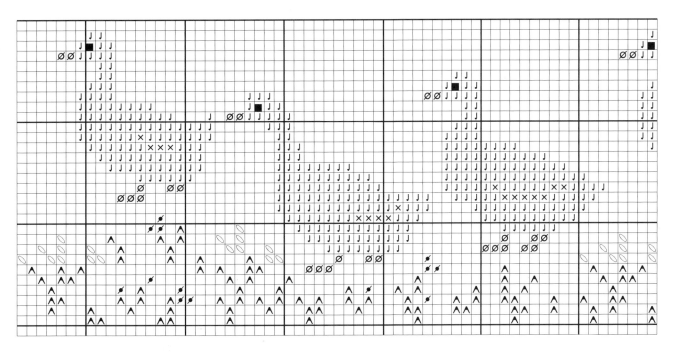

HEARTS AND FLOWERS TOWEL BORDER

γou can buy Aida ready-made into border strips, or use ordinary Aida and turn under the edges before you stitch it to the towel. This design can be varied by using different colours from those given in the chart.

Material
Aida with 5½ stitches per cm (13½ stitches per in)

Cutting size
8cm (3¼in) deep

Finished size
5cm (2in) deep

Thread
DMC embroidery thread. Use 2 strands in the needle

Finishing
See page 18 for instructions on making a bath towel edging

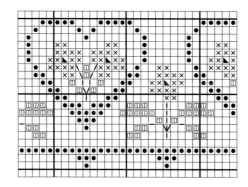

◤	580	dark green
⊞	703	light green
●	891	red
⊠	62	light rose
– –	580	dark green (back stitch)

BLACKBERRY TOWEL BORDER

*T*o make a matching set, stitch borders for the towels and isolate part of the design as a motif for smaller items such as face cloths. Work your family initial or individual initials to match the towel from the letters in Chapter 4.

Material
White Aida with 5½ stitches
  per cm (13½ stitches per in)

Cutting size
10cm (4in) deep

Finished size
5.5cm (2¼in) deep

Thread
DMC embroidery thread. Use
  2 strands in the needle

Finishing
See page 18 for instructions on
  making a bath towel edging

■	310	black
●	902	dark red
⊟	3803	red
⊻	543	beige
◣	3346	dark green
◙	989	medium green
◥	471	light green
◈	733	dull green
L	3817	light blue-green
∞∞∞∞	553	lilac (back stitch)
— —	471	light green (back stitch)

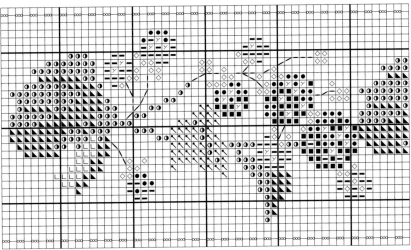

TULIP TABLE RUNNER

A strong yellow has been chosen for this project, but with the variety of tulip colours now available, you could select almost any colour to match your own kitchen or dining room decor.

Material
White Aida with 5½ stitches per cm (13½ stitches per in)

Cutting size
33 x 45cm (13 x 17½in)

Finished size
28 x 40cm (11 x 16in)

Thread
DMC embroidery thread. Use 2 strands in the needle

Finishing
See page 17 for instructions on making a table runner

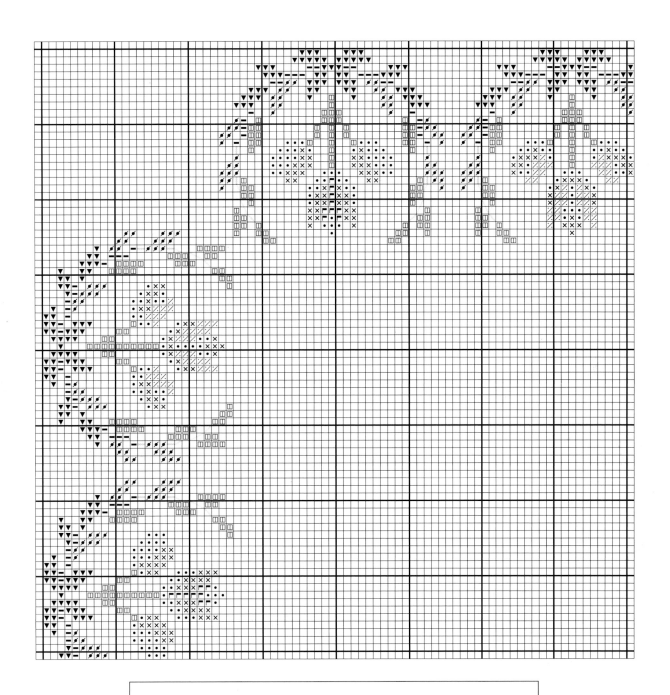

▼	904 dark green	●	972 dark yellow
✓	906 medium green	✗	444 medium yellow
▥	907 light green	◹	307 light yellow
▬	731 dull green	∞∞∞∞	731 dull green
▭	971 orange		(back stitch)

NOTICE BOARD WITH FLOWERS

*P*erfect for the gardener to keep their notes on planting or other garden jobs, and even to pin their seed packets to keep them safe and ready for sewing.

Materials
Beige Aida with 4½ stitches
  per cm (11 stitches per in)
33 x 48cm (13 x 19in) stiff card
  or corkboard

Cutting size
40 x 55cm (16 x 21½in)

Finished size
33 x 48cm (13 x 19in)

Thread
DMC embroidery thread. Use 3
  strands in the needle

Finishing
See page 16 for instructions on
  making a notice board

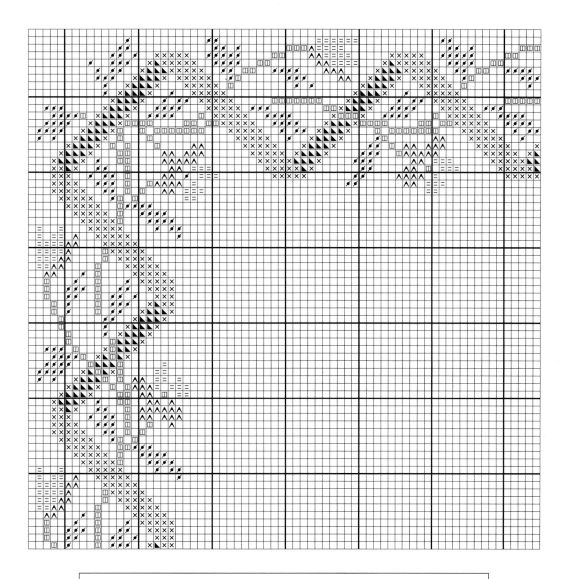

	931 dark grey-blue		471 light green
	827 light blue		922 rust
	988 dark green		977 light rust

NOTICE BOARD WITH FISH

An amusing gift for an angler or someone living by the sea, you can bind all four edges in a bias strip if you prefer.

Materials
White Aida with 4½ stitches per cm (11 stitches per in)
40 x 60cm (16 x 24in) stiff card or corkboard
2.1m (2¼yds) bias binding

Cutting size
45 x 65cm (17½ x 25½in)

Finished size
40 x 60cm (16 x 24in)

Thread
DMC embroidery thread. Use 3 strands in the needle

Finishing
Stitch the bias binding round three sides of the embroidery, measuring carefully so that it is positioned on the edge of the board and mitring the corners (see page 10). Then see page 16 for instructions on making a notice board

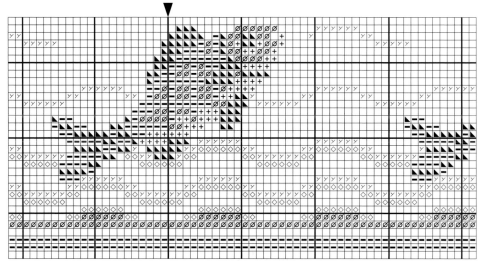

◣	791	dark blue
⊟	825	medium blue
⊘	518	light blue
⊞	519	lightest blue
◈	563	light turquoise
⊡	369	light green

3
MOTIFS

You can find inspiration from almost anywhere for motifs to use in cross stitch embroidery: flowers, birds, animals, children, even abstract patterns.

Think about the overall shape of the motif so that it has a pleasing symmetry, and remember that the space around the motif works as part of the design, so don't overcrowd an area, or bring an associated border in too close to the motif. By repeating single motifs, or a collection of themed motifs, you can create an overall design. You can also combine motifs very effectively with borders, as you can see in this section, to create attractive and versatile designs.

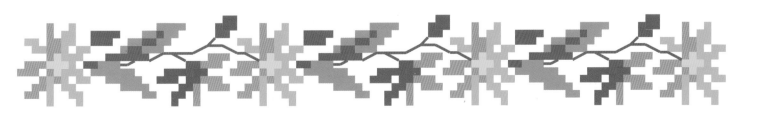

FRUITS

$\mathcal{T}$he two borders and range of fruit motifs can be used for a variety of projects, especially for the kitchen or dining room. If you want to make this as a single wall hanging, select and continue just one of the borders.

Material
Aida with $5\frac{1}{2}$ stitches per cm ($13\frac{1}{2}$ stitches per in)

Cutting size
34 x 30cm ($13\frac{1}{2}$ x 12in)

Finished size
25 x 21cm (10 x $8\frac{1}{4}$in)

Border widths
1cm ($\frac{1}{2}$in)

Motif sizes
Cherries 7 x 6 ($2\frac{3}{4}$ x $2\frac{1}{2}$in)
Blackcurrants 4 x 2.5 ($1\frac{1}{2}$ x 1in)
Bilberries 7 x 5cm ($2\frac{3}{4}$ x 2in)
Strawberries 7 x 5.5cm ($2\frac{3}{4}$ x $2\frac{1}{4}$in)
Pear 5 x 4cm (2 x $1\frac{1}{2}$in)
Grapes 8 x 7cm ($3\frac{1}{4}$ x $2\frac{3}{4}$in)

Thread
DMC embroidery thread. Use 2 strands in the needle

Finishing
See page 17 for instructions on making a wall hanging

Cherries

◣	3345	dark green
⊟	3346	medium green
◪	470	light green
⊠	471	lightest green
✳	611	brown
◤	498	dark red
•	309	medium red
＋	950	light beige

Blackcurrants

■	310	black
◪	920	dark red
◨	223	light dull red
✳	611	brown
▽	734	light beige
—	734	light beige (back stitch)

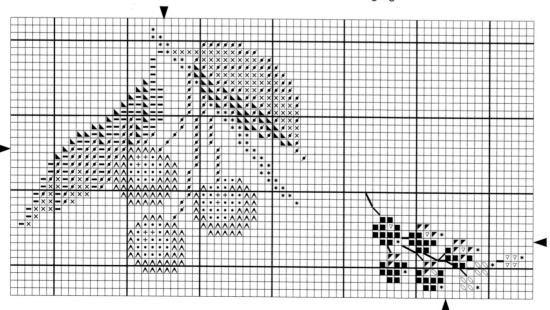

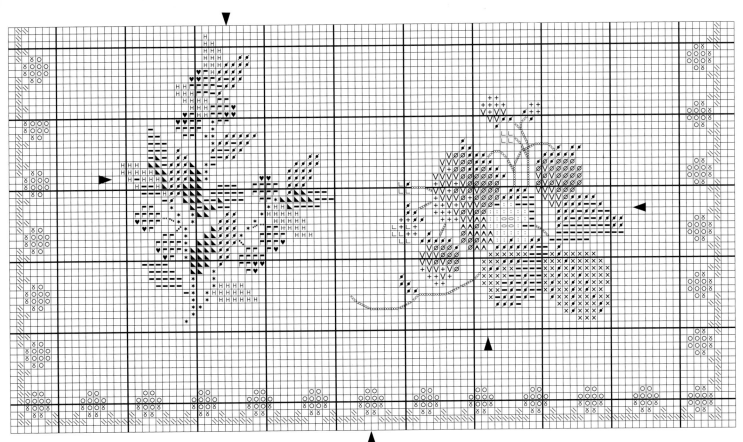

Border

⊠	905	green
⊗	891	dark rose
⊙	893	light rose

Bilberries

◣	3345	dark green
⊟	3346	medium green
▨	470	light green
H	733	dull green
♥	336	dark blue
⊡	797	medium blue
✳	611	brown
•••••	3350	dark red (back stitch)

Strawberries

⊟	3346	dark green	⊻	351	light red
▨	470	medium green	+	950	light dull rose
⊠	471	light green	⊟	973	yellow
L	472	lightest green	⋮		white
⊼	498	dark red	∞∞∞∞	471	light green (back stitch)
⊘	349	medium red			

Border

⊞	906	green
⊙	893	rose
⊡	445	light yellow
—	906	green (back stitch)

Grapes

⊟	3346	dark green
◪	470	medium green
⊠	471	light green
◧	831	tobacco brown
◺	733	dull green
Y	734	light dull green
⊟	372	beige
J	712	light beige
▼	550	dark lilac
⊗	3803	red
◺	223	light dull red
∘∘∘∘∘∘	372	beige (back stitch)

Pear

◣	3345	dark green
⊟	3346	medium green
⊠	471	light green
■	610	brown
●	782	light brown
⦀	729	golden
◇	3821	light golden

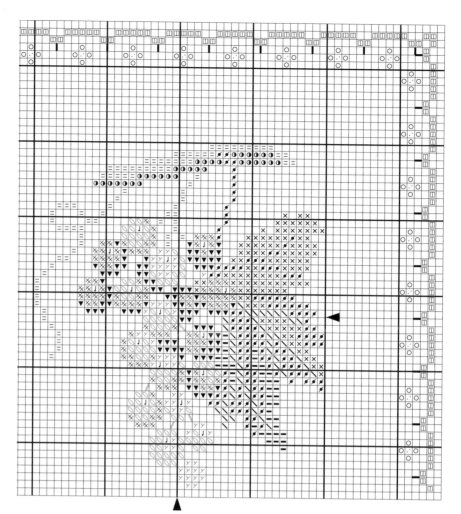

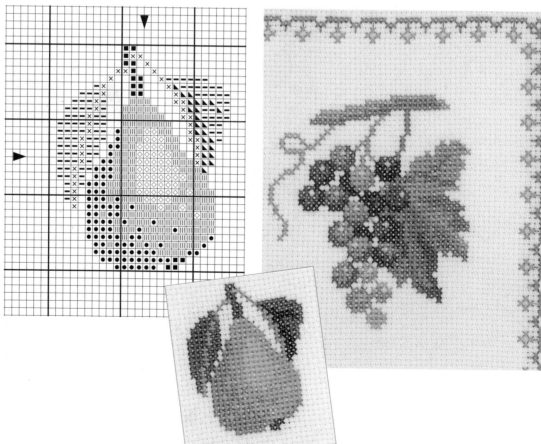

BRIAR ROSES AND ORNAMENTAL THORNS

*T*he clear shapes of the briar rose, *Rosa rubiginosa*, the thorn bush, *Crataegus*, and the popular privet, *Ligustrum*, make excellent motifs for all kinds of projects.

Material
Aida with 5½ stitches per cm (13½ stitches per in)

Border widths
Top 2.5cm (1in)
Bottom 4cm (1½in)

Motif sizes
Briar rose 6 x 5cm
  (2½ x 2in)
Ornamental thorn
  5 x 4.5cm (2 x 1¾in)
Privet 9.5 x 6cm
  (3¾ x 2½in)

Thread
DMC embroidery thread.
  Use 2 strands in the
  needle

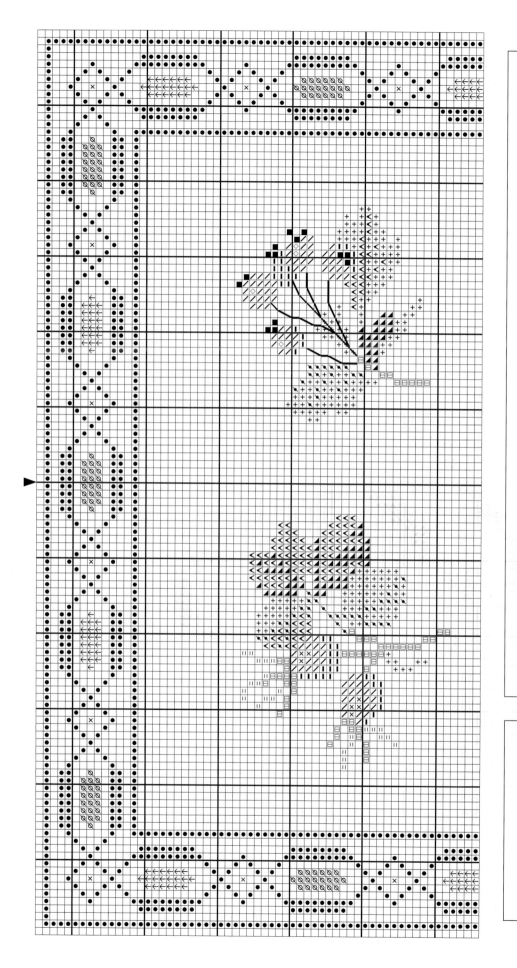

Briar rose and ornamental thorn

◣ 3346 dark green
◀ 470 light green
▮ 498 dark red
◿ 349 medium red

☒ 947 orange
⊟ 611 dark beige
⊟ 648 light grey
◼ 732 dull green

⊞ 734 light dull green
■ 310 black
◇ 950 light pale rose
— 611 dark beige

Border

● 300 brown
☒ 947 orange
⊘ 3814 turquoise
← 907 green

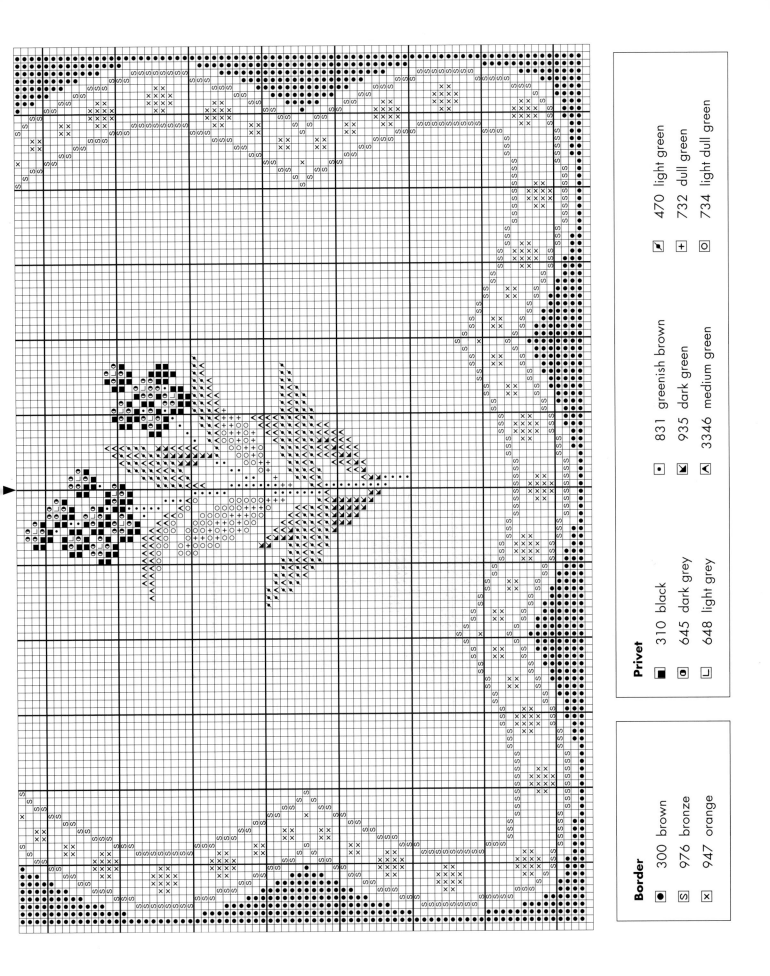

Privet

■	310	black
◙	645	dark grey
∟	648	light grey
•	831	greenish brown
◪	935	dark green
◤	3346	medium green
◪	470	light green
+	732	dull green
○	734	light dull green

Border

●	300	brown
S	976	bronze
×	947	orange

WREATHS

*I*nitials can be very attractive when combined with a wreath design based on flowers, patterns, or something relevant to the recipient, if you are embroidering a gift. This border would make an excellent design for a table runner.

Material
Linen with 8 threads per cm (20 threads per in)

Border width
3cm (1¼in)

Motif sizes
H 2 x 2cm (¾ x ¾in)
S 4 x 4cm (1½ x 1½in)
R 12 x 14cm (4¾ x 5½in)
B 6 x 8cm (2½ x 3¼cm)
Small B 2 x 4cm (¾ x 1½in)
G 2 x 3cm (¾ x 1¼in)

Thread
DMC embroidery thread. Use 3 strands in the needle

●	987	green
▥	3347	light green
◪	580	yellow-green
⊠	581	light yellow-green
▼	3803	darkest red
⊟	3350	dark red
◩	309	medium red
⌐	893	light red
■	310	black
◌	3820	yellow
◣	552	dark lilac
◪	553	medium lilac
+	3608	light lilac
✳	3746	dark blue
N	340	medium blue
◨	341	light blue
∿∿	987	green (back stitch)
—	580	yellow-green (back stitch)
⋯⋯	3803	darkest red (back stitch)

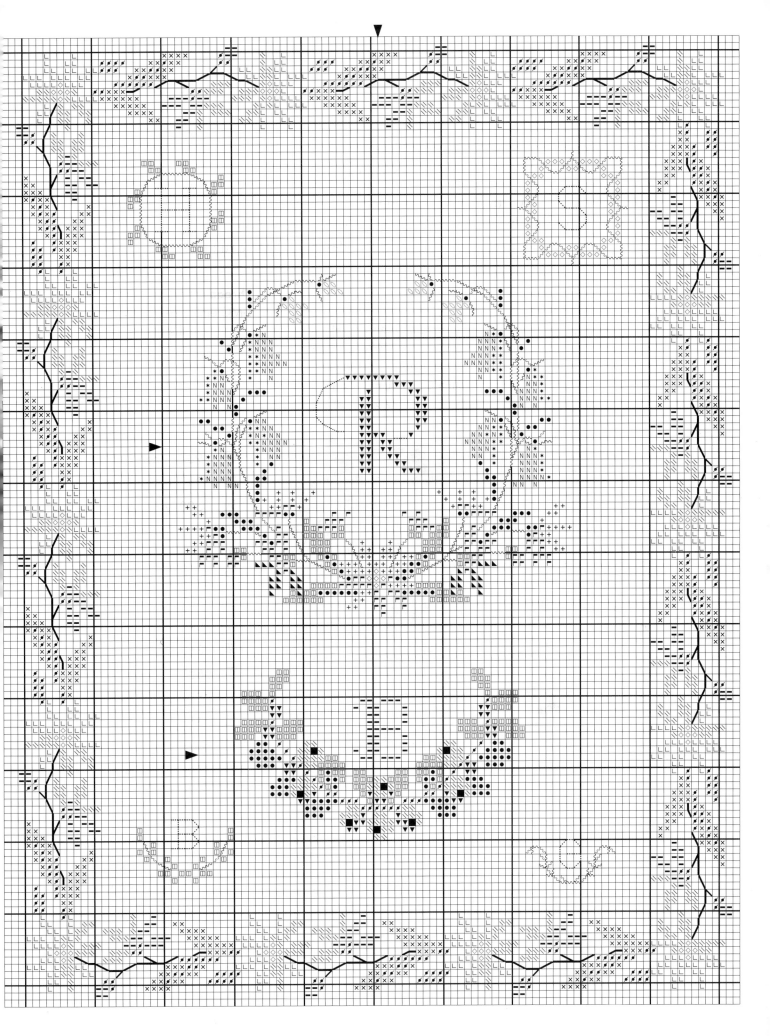

FAVOURITE FLOWERS

*M*atch threads carefully to the colours of your chosen flowers. Using a range of subtle tones gives the delicate effect of shading on the petals and the leaves.

Material
Linen with 8 threads per cm
  (20 threads per in)

Cutting size
45 x 40cm (17½ x 16in)

Finished size
37 x 30cm (14¾ x 12in)

Border width
4cm (1½in)

Motif sizes
Dog rose
  6 x 6cm (2½ x 2½in)
Fuschia
  7 x 6cm (1¾ x 2½in)
Blue fantasy
  6 x 3cm (2½ x 1¼in)
Aster
  6 x 6cm
  (2½ x 2½in)
Rose fantasy
  6 x 3cm
  (2½ x 1¼in)
Forget-me-not
  8 x 7cm
  (3¼ x 2¾in)
Violet
  8 x 8cm
  (3¼ x 3¼in)

Thread
DMC embroidery thread. Use 3 strands in the needle

Finishing
See page 17 for instructions on making a wall hanging

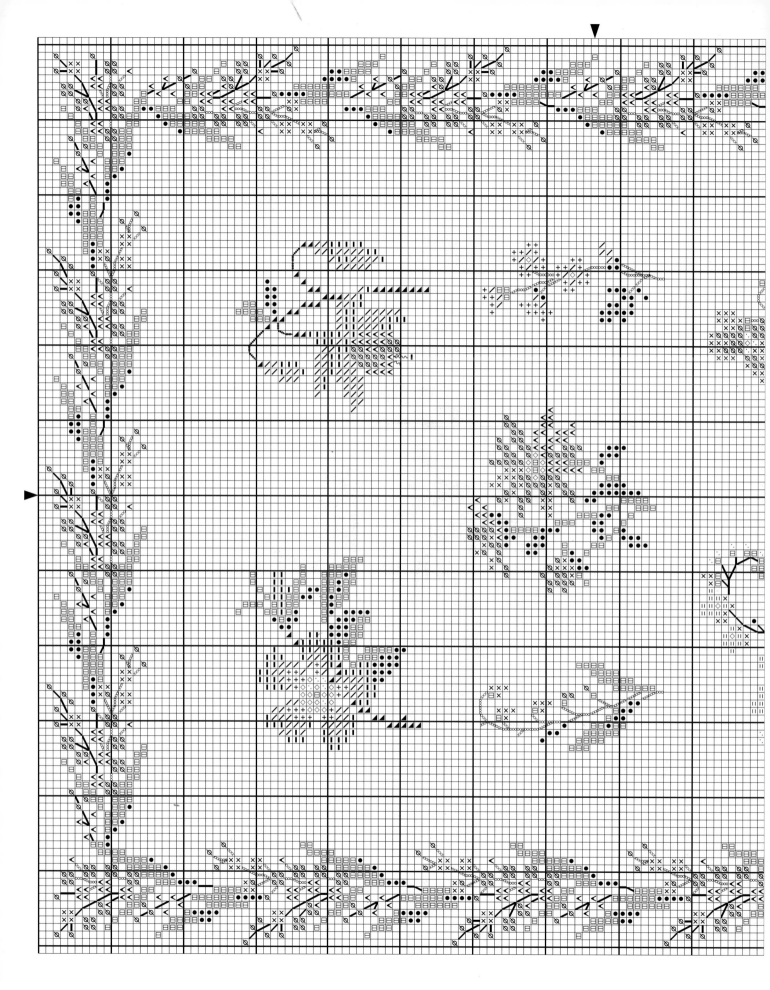

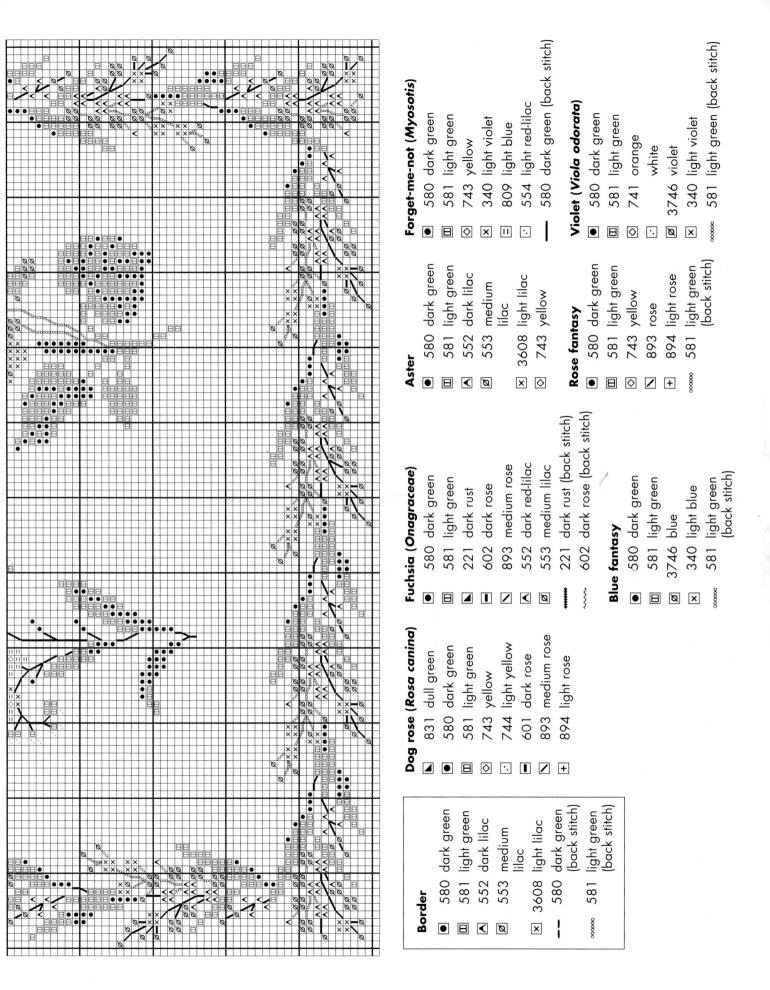

Forget-me-not (*Myosotis*)
- ● 580 dark green
- ⊟ 581 light green
- ◇ 743 yellow
- ✕ 340 light violet
- ⊟ 809 light blue
- ⸬ 554 light red-lilac
- ▬ 580 dark green (back stitch)

Violet (*Viola odorata*)
- ● 580 dark green
- ⊟ 581 light green
- ◇ 741 orange
- ⸬ white
- ⊘ 3746 violet
- ✕ 340 light violet
- ∞∞∞ 581 light green (back stitch)

Aster
- ● 580 dark green
- ⊟ 581 light green
- ◪ 552 dark lilac
- ⊘ 553 medium lilac
- ✕ 3608 light lilac
- ◇ 743 yellow

Rose fantasy
- ● 580 dark green
- ⊟ 581 light green
- ◇ 743 yellow
- ◿ 893 rose
- ✚ 894 light rose
- ∞∞∞ 581 light green (back stitch)

Fuchsia (*Onagraceae*)
- ● 580 dark green
- ⊟ 581 light green
- ◣ 221 dark rust
- ▮ 602 dark rose
- ◿ 893 medium rose
- ◪ 552 dark red-lilac
- ⊘ 553 medium lilac
- ▬▬ 221 dark rust (back stitch)
- ∿ 602 dark rose (back stitch)

Blue fantasy
- ● 580 dark green
- ⊟ 581 light green
- ⊘ 3746 blue
- ✕ 340 light blue
- ∞∞∞ 581 light green (back stitch)

Dog rose (*Rosa canina*)
- ◪ 831 dull green
- ● 580 dark green
- ⊟ 581 light green
- ◇ 743 yellow
- ⸬ 744 light yellow
- ▮ 601 dark rose
- ◿ 893 medium rose
- ✚ 894 light rose

Border
- ● 580 dark green
- ⊟ 581 light green
- ◪ 552 dark lilac
- ⊘ 553 medium lilac
- ✕ 3608 light lilac
- ▬ 580 dark green (back stitch)
- ∞∞∞ 581 light green (back stitch)

CHILDREN

*G*reat inspiration for samplers, remember to personalize any people you include in your embroidery. Finish the features over the flesh-coloured cross stitch with a single strand of black or brown thread.

Material
Aida with 5½ stitches per cm (13½ stitches per in)

Cutting size
30 x 25cm (12 x 10in)

Finished size
25 x 20cm (10 x 8in)

Border widths
Flowers 2.5cm (1in)
Children 3cm (1¼in)

Motif sizes
Children 5.5 x 2.5cm (2¼ x 1in)
Footballers 5.5 x 4cm (2¼ x 1½in)
Flowers 4.5 x 6cm (1¾ x 2½in)
Baby 3 x 3cm (1¼ x 1¼in)
Woman 5 x 5cm (2 x 2in)

Thread
DMC embroidery thread. Use 2 strands in the needle

Finishing
See page 17 for instructions on making a wall hanging

◿	987	dark green
▥	906	green
⊗	958	turquoise
◺	517	medium blue
⊠	799	light blue
●	791	dark lavender blue
⊡	3746	lavender blue
◹	209	light lilac
■	310	black
▼	300	dark red-brown
▨	919	rust
⊘	435	bronze
⊟	3779	flesh
◩	977	apricot
➕	743	yellow
⬚	606	bright red
▧	3805	rose
∞∞∞∞	906	green (back stitch)
▬▬	300	dark red-brown (back stitch)
⌇⌇	435	bronze (back stitch)

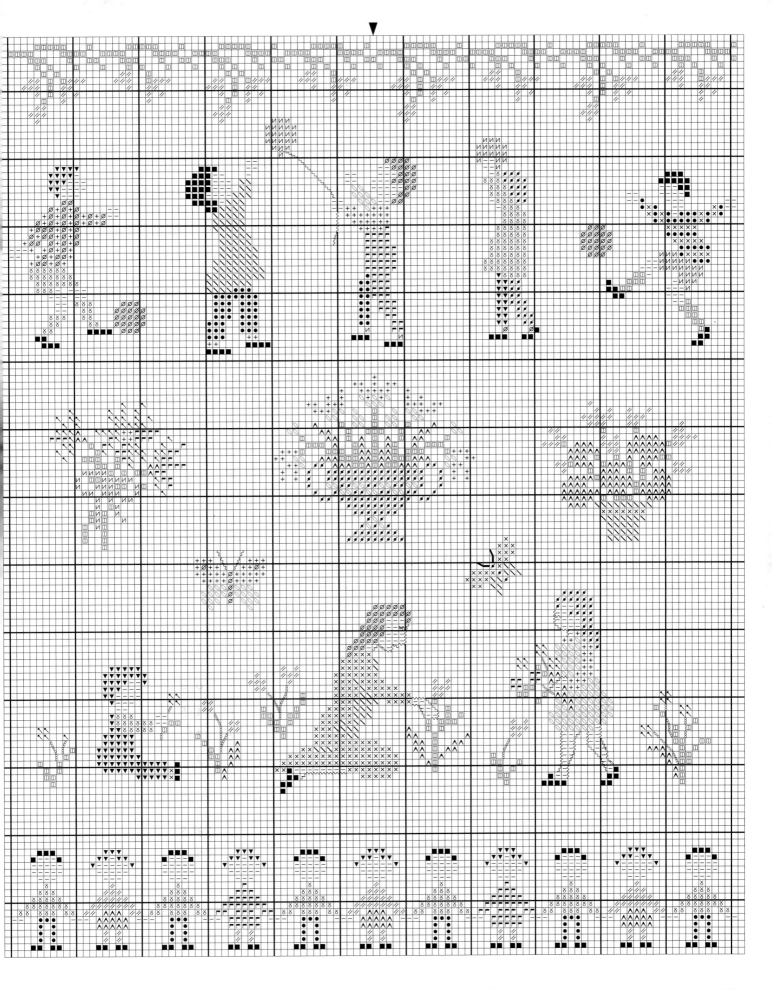

HOMES AND ANIMALS

A ready-made design for pet-lovers, substitute the details of your own pets to make an attractive sampler or use the motifs individually when you are creating your own work.

Material
Aida with 5 stitches per cm
  (13 stitches per in)

Cutting size
30 x 25cm (12 x 10in)

Finished size
25 x 20cm (10 x 8in)

Border width
2cm (¾in)

Motif sizes
Houses 8 x 15cm (3¼ x 6in)
Duck 2 x 2cm (¾ x ¾in)
Swan 3 x 3cm (1¼ x 1¼in)
Rabbit 4 x 4cm (1½ x 1½in)
Dog 4 x 5cm (1½ x 2in)
Cat 4 x 5cm (1½ x 2in)

Thread
DMC embroidery thread. Use 2
strands in the needle

Finishing
See page 17 for instructions on
  making a wall hanging

Symbol	Code	Colour
■	310	black
⬤	646	dark grey
⋅		white
▼	869	dark brown
Ø	422	light brown
⊞	739	light beige
◪	921	rust
◩	741	orange
⊠	950	flesh
◇	676	light golden
⊟	797	dark blue
⊞	806	medium blue
▽	3753	light blue
◮	703	green
⊟	907	light green
—	646	dark grey (back stitch)
∘∘∘∘∘∘	921	rust (back stitch)
‹‹‹‹‹	598	light turquoise (back stitch)
∿∿∿	703	green (back stitch)

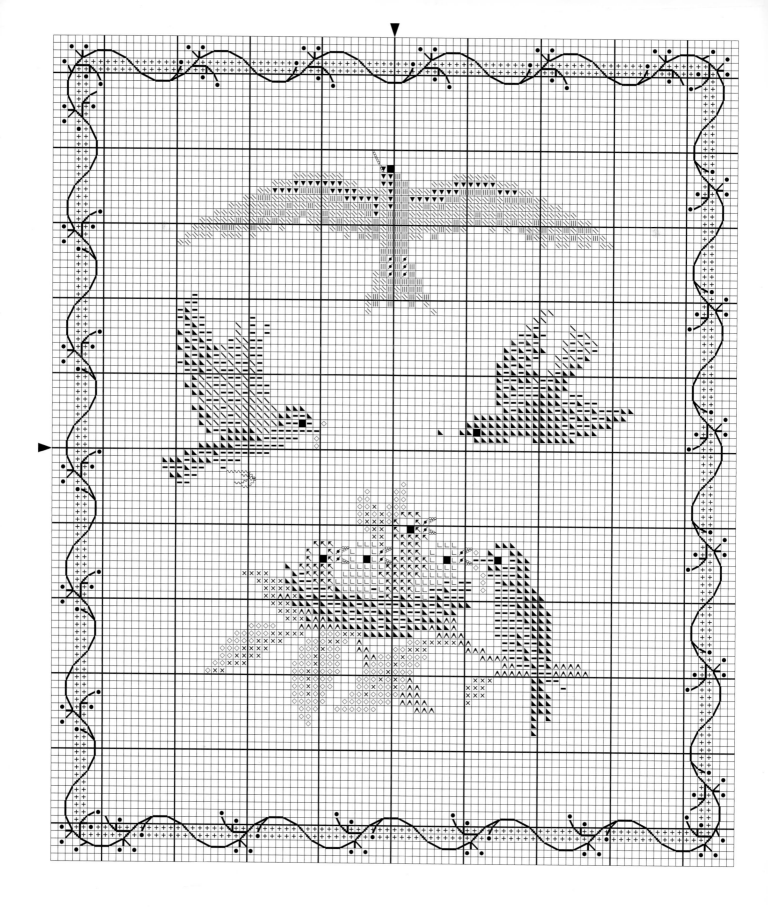

FLYING AND FEEDING BIRDS

$\mathcal{W}$atching birds in the garden or looking at nature books will give you inspiration and detail for bird embroideries. Accurate details, such as the shape of the claws and beak, make all the difference.

Border

⊙	791	dark blue
⊞	734	golden
—	580	green

▼	926	dark dull blue
⦀	932	medium dull blue
◩	3753	light dull blue
■	310	black
◪	720	orange
◣	830	brown
⊟	370	dark beige
◲	642	light beige
▲	987	dark green
⊠	906	medium green
◌	907	light green
◥	972	dark yellow
∟	444	light yellow
∘∘∘∘∘	720	orange (back stitch)
⌇⌇⌇	830	brown (back stitch)

Material
Linen with 8 threads per cm
(20 threads per in)

Cutting size
33 x 30cm (13 x 12in)

Finished size
27 x 24cm (10¾ x 9½in)

Border width
2cm (¾in)

Motif sizes
Gull 5.5 x 15cm (3¼ x 6in)
Flying bird 6 x 6cm (2½ x 2½in)
Nest 8 x 12.5cm (3 x 4¾in)

Thread
DMC embroidery thread. Use 3
strands in the needle

Finishing
See page 17 for instructions on
making a wall hanging

COLOURFUL BIRDS

*C*olourful birds make particularly good subjects for embroidery. Think about the foliage you stitch with them and choose something which the birds visit for nesting or to find food.

Material
Linen with 8 threads per cm
  (20 threads per in)

Cutting size
45 x 38cm (17½ x 15in)

Finished size
40 x 33cm (16 x 13in)

Border width
6cm (1½in)

Motif size
10 x 9 cm (4 x 3½in)

Thread
DMC embroidery thread. Use 3
  strands in the needle

Finishing
See page 17 for instructions on
  making a wall hanging

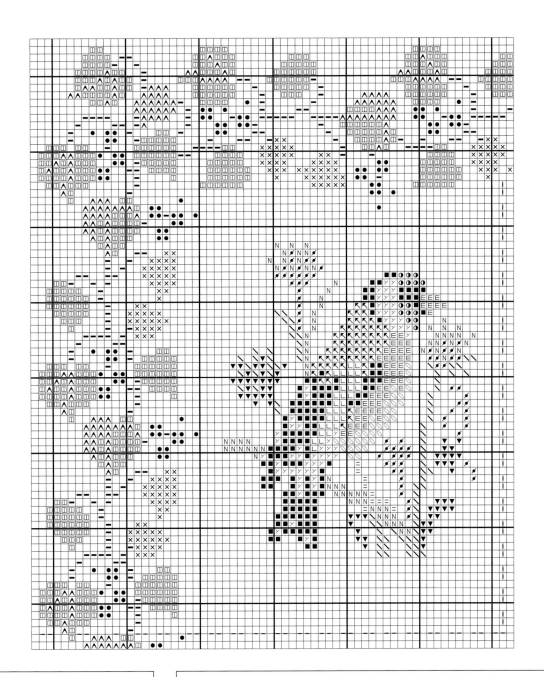

Border

▭	3012	dull green
Ⓐ	3346	dark green
▣	906	medium green
⊠	907	light green
⊡	309	red

Goldfinch (*Carduelis carduelis*)

■	310	black		Ⓝ	581	green
⊟	3022	grey		◤	435	red-brown
⊻		white		Ⓔ	437	light brown
▼	3781	dark brown		◲	738	lightest brown
◪	3790	brown		⊡	817	red
◳	370	dull green		Ⓛ	743	gold

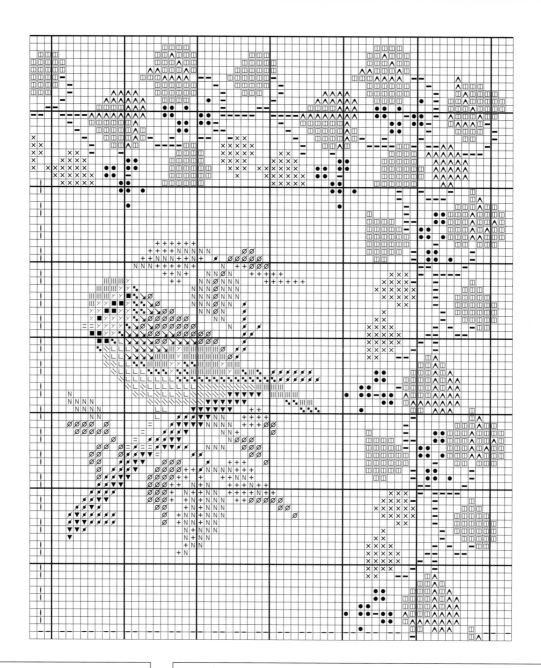

Border

▬	3012	dull green
▲	3346	dark green
⊞	906	medium green
✕	907	light green
●	309	red

Blue tit (*Parus caeruleus*)

■	310	black		◿	3815	blue-green
⊟	3022	grey		⊘	988	green
⊠		white		✛	471	light green
▼	3021	dark brown		N	581	yellow-green
◪	3790	brown		◺	834	golden
▞	930	dark dull blue		⌊	743	yellow
⦀	3760	blue				

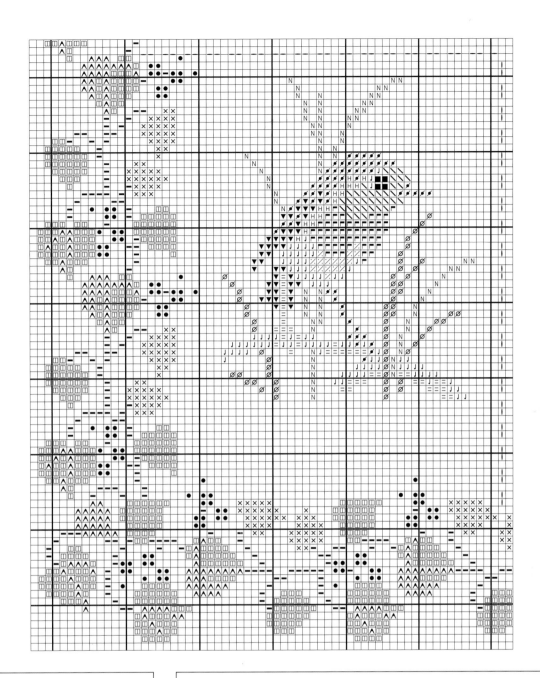

Border

⊟	3012	dull green
⬛	3346	dark green
⊡	906	medium green
⊠	907	light green
⬤	309	red

Robin (*Erithacus rubecula*)

◼	310	black		⊡	921	rust
▼	3021	dark brown		◹	3776	light rust
◪	3790	light brown		H	926	dull blue
⊟	3022	dark grey		⊘	988	green
⅃	648	medium grey		N	581	yellow-green
⬕	3024	light grey				

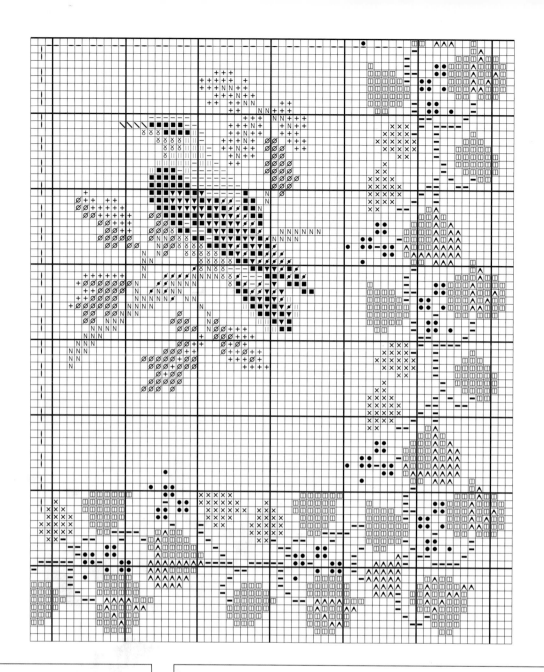

Border

▬	3012	dull green
◪	3346	dark green
⊞	906	medium green
☒	907	light green
⊡	309	red

Golden oriole (*Oriolus oriolus*)

■	310	black	⊞	3820	medium yellow
▼	3021	dark brown	▬	743	light yellow
◪	3790	light brown	∅	988	green
◣	3776	rust	N	581	yellow-green
⊠	783	dark yellow	+	471	light green

4

ALPHABETS

*I*nitials are a wonderful way to make an embroidery completely unique and special, particularly if you are making gifts. You can sew them on to all kinds of material, either direct or by using waste canvas (see page 10). A favourite sweater will get a new lease of life with a monogram – or even a motif such as a flower or a football player for the sports fan. Vary the size of the initials you are using by choosing a canvas in the right size.

You can also link two or more initials together, perhaps with a motif, as you can see in the final project in this chapter.

SIMPLE ALPHABETS

$\mathcal{M}$ake an alphabet sampler, or select the letters you need as initials or text to decorate your embroidery. Letters are best spaced visually, so plan out lettering on graph paper before starting to stitch. You will need more space between straight-sided letters than between diagonal letters.

Material
White Aida with 5½ stitches per cm (13½ stitches per in)

Cutting size
35 x 30cm (14 x 12in)

Finished size
30 x 25cm (12 x 10in)

Thread
DMC embroidery thread. Use 2 strands in the needle

Finishing
See page 17 for instructions on making a wall hanging

⊞	947	orange
■	321	red
⊙	906	green
▲	93 or 826	blue
—	321	red (back stitch)
∾∾∾	906	green (back stitch)
∿∿	93 or 826	blue (back stitch)

CURSIVE ALPHABETS

*I*f your design is more ornate, you may want to use a script letter to complement the style of the motif or border. In this case, the flowing script is combined with a very simple border which sets it off to best effect.

Material
White Aida with 5½ stitches per cm
(13½ stitches per in)

Cutting size
38 x 31cm (15 x 12½in)

Finished size
33 x 26cm (13 x 10¼in)

Thread
DMC embroidery thread. Use 2 strands in the needle

Finishing
See page 17 for instructions on making a wall hanging

▲	3814	turquoise
⊘	906	green
⌐	3819	light yellow-green
●	333	blue
◣	309	red
☒	783	gold
∞∞∞∞	3814	turquoise (back stitch)
—	333	blue (back stitch)

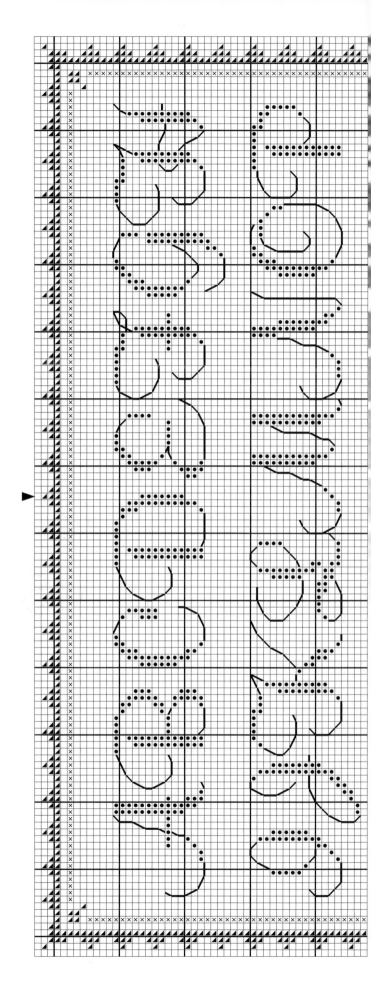

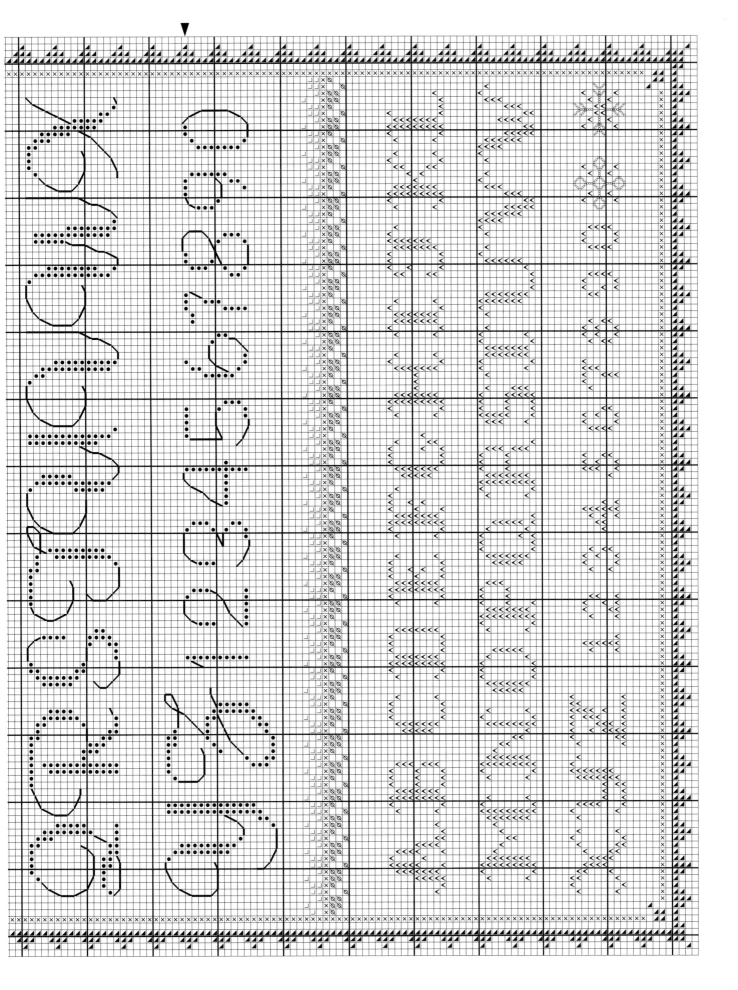

ABCDEFGH
IJKLMNOP
QRSTUVWX
YZ 1234567890

ABCDEFGHIJKL
MNOPQRSTUVW
XYZ 1234567890 ❈ ❉

INITIALS A TO Z

*U*se colours to suit your particular design and add appropriate initials to personalize gifts. The main measurements for cutting and finished sizes given are for the largest letters. Individual motif sizes are given beneath the appropriate charts.

Material
White Aida with 4½ stitches per cm (11 stitches per in)

Cutting size
About 13 x 14cm (5 x 5½in)

Finished size
About 7.5 x 10cm (3 x 4in)

Thread
DMC embroidery thread. Use 3 strands in the needle

☒	892	red
⊙	797	blue
– –	907	green (back stitch)

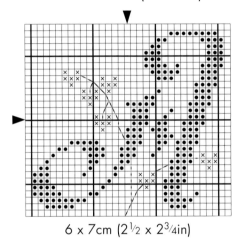

6 x 7cm (2½ x 2¾in)

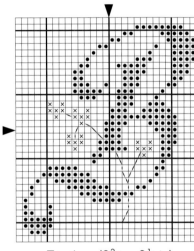

7 x 6cm (2¾ x 2½in)

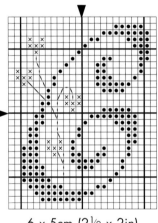

6 x 5cm (2½ x 2in)

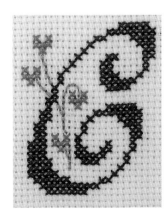

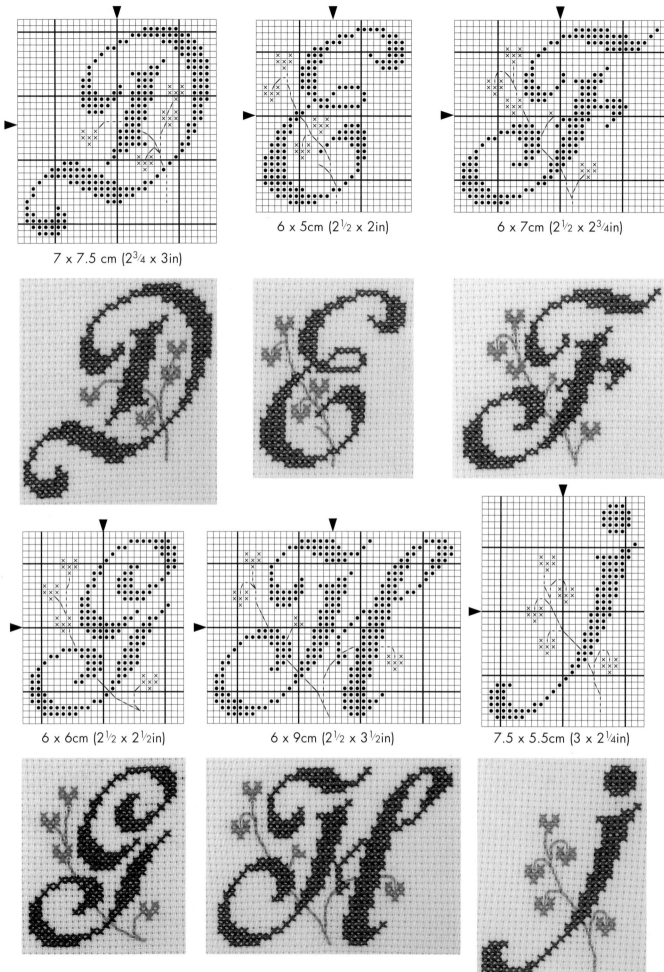

7 x 7.5 cm (2³/₄ x 3in)

6 x 5cm (2¹/₂ x 2in)

6 x 7cm (2¹/₂ x 2³/₄in)

6 x 6cm (2¹/₂ x 2¹/₂in)

6 x 9cm (2¹/₂ x 3¹/₂in)

7.5 x 5.5cm (3 x 2¹/₄in)

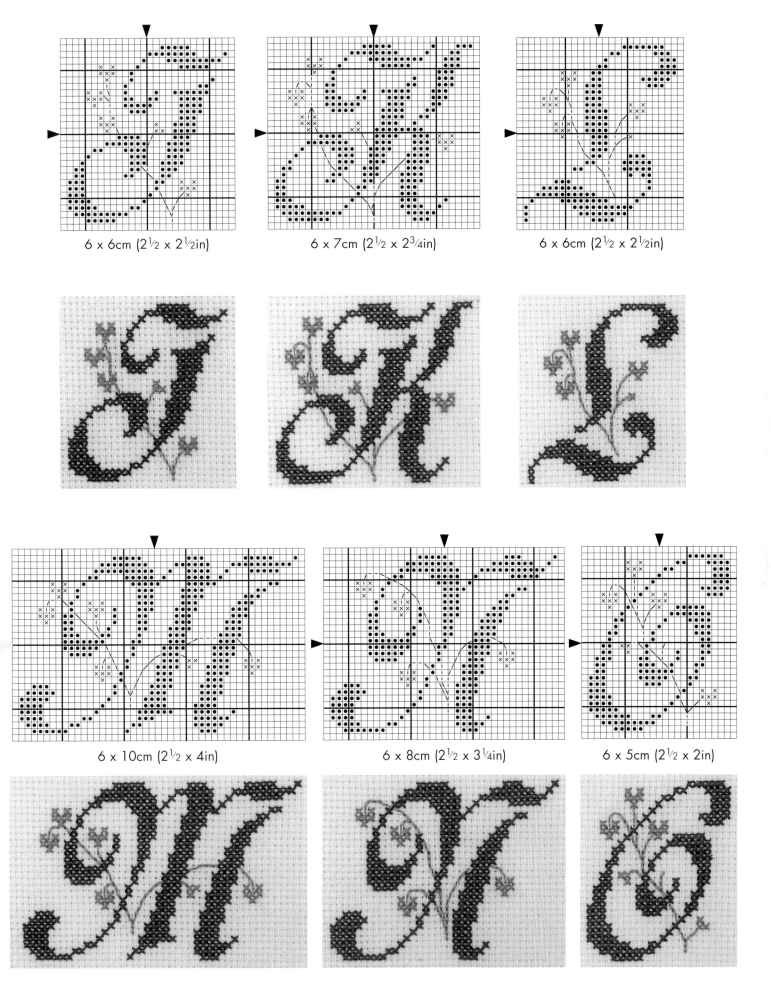

6 x 6cm (2½ x 2½in)   6 x 7cm (2½ x 2¾in)   6 x 6cm (2½ x 2½in)

6 x 10cm (2½ x 4in)   6 x 8cm (2½ x 3¼in)   6 x 5cm (2½ x 2in)

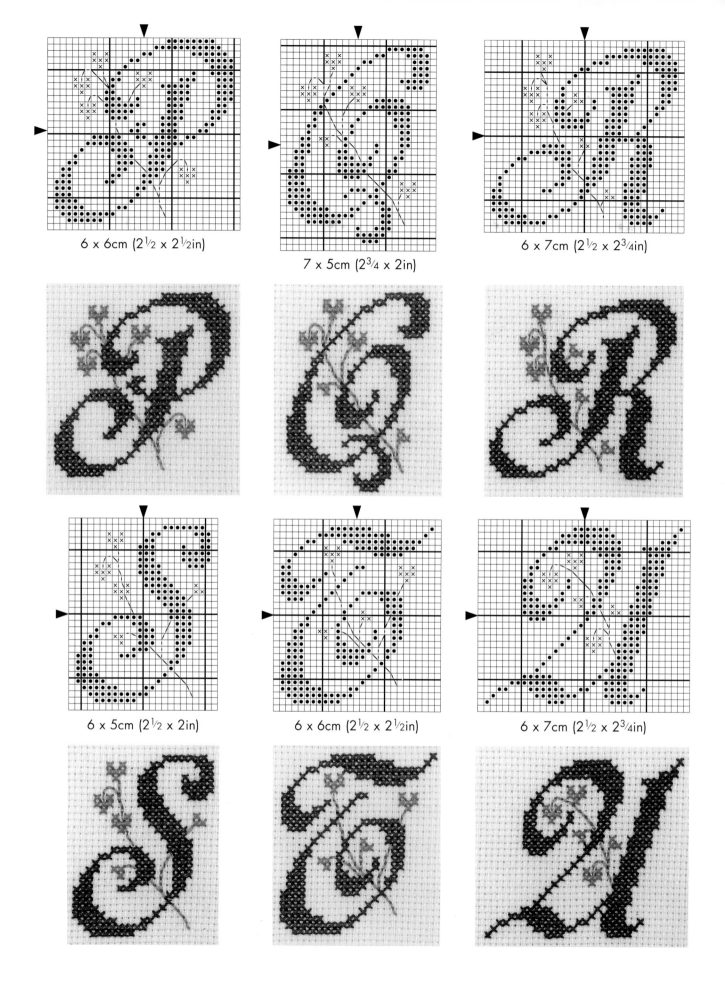

6 x 6cm (2¹⁄₂ x 2¹⁄₂in)

7 x 5cm (2³⁄₄ x 2in)

6 x 7cm (2¹⁄₂ x 2³⁄₄in)

6 x 5cm (2¹⁄₂ x 2in)

6 x 6cm (2¹⁄₂ x 2¹⁄₂in)

6 x 7cm (2¹⁄₂ x 2³⁄₄in)

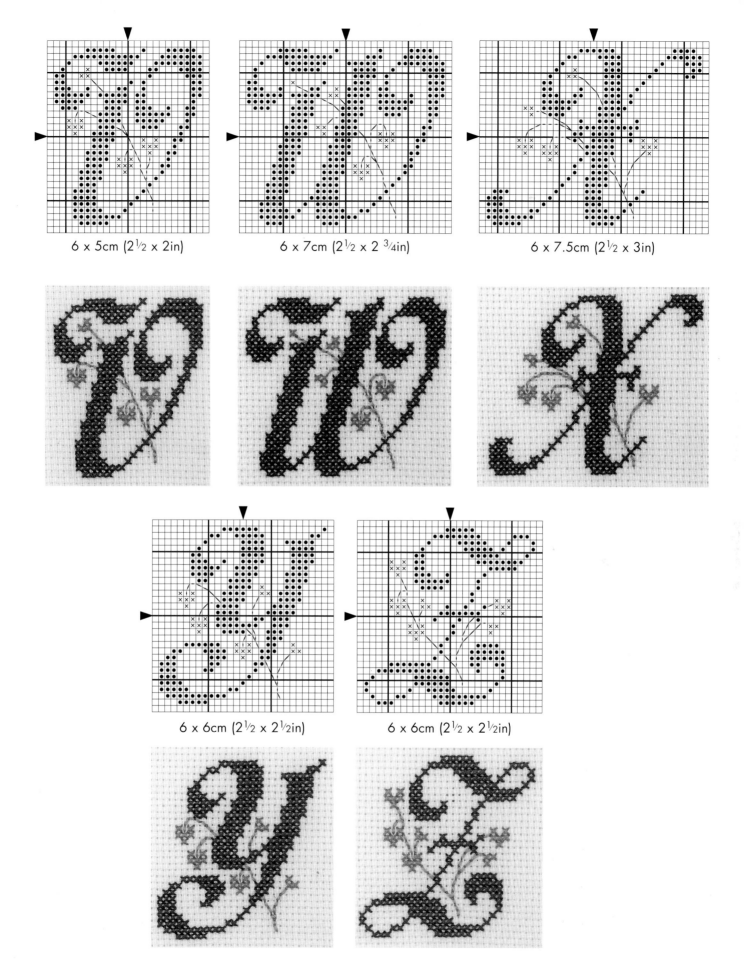

6 x 5cm (2½ x 2in)   6 x 7cm (2½ x 2¾in)   6 x 7.5cm (2½ x 3in)

6 x 6cm (2½ x 2½in)   6 x 6cm (2½ x 2½in)

MONOGRAMS

$\mathcal{T}$o link two initials, first draw them individually on tracing paper, then move them around until you have a pleasing arrangement. Copy them on to squared paper and add the flower vine to link the leaves together.

Material
White Aida with 4½ stitches
   per cm (11 stitches per in)

Cutting size
14 x 14cm (5½ x 5½in)

Finished size
9 x 9cm (3½ x 3½in)

Thread
DMC embroidery thread. Use
   3 strands in the needle

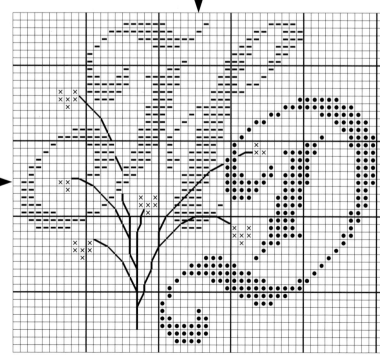

⊡	806	blue
⊟	958	turquoise
⊠	3806	rose
—	906	light green
		(back stitch)

5

ZODIAC DESIGNS

These zodiac designs are made up as plate liners, but the designs can just as easily be used for greetings cards, to embroider on a T-shirt, or as motifs on place mats or table runners. The star border is common to all the projects, and you can follow the pattern, or replace it with your own. You may like to think about using colours appropriate to the sign: blues and greens for water signs such as Cancer and Pisces, for example; reds and oranges for the fire signs such as Leo and Sagittarius, and so on. The star motifs could be replaced with an appropriate symbol: perhaps a Moon for Cancer with its lunar influences, or a flower for Virgo. A few ideas are suggested in the introductions.

ARIES

*T*he first sign of the zodiac is a fire sign associated with Mars and the bloodstone, so red would be a good colour choice for the boder. Aries is also sometimes associated with growth and new life, so a plant motif would also be appropriate.

Material
Linen with 10 threads per cm
(25 threads per in)

Cutting size
22 x 22cm (8½ x 8½in)

Finished size
15 x 15cm (6 x 6in)

Thread
DMC embroidery thread or metallic thread. Use 2 strands in the needle

Finishing
See page 19 for instructions on making rectangular table linen

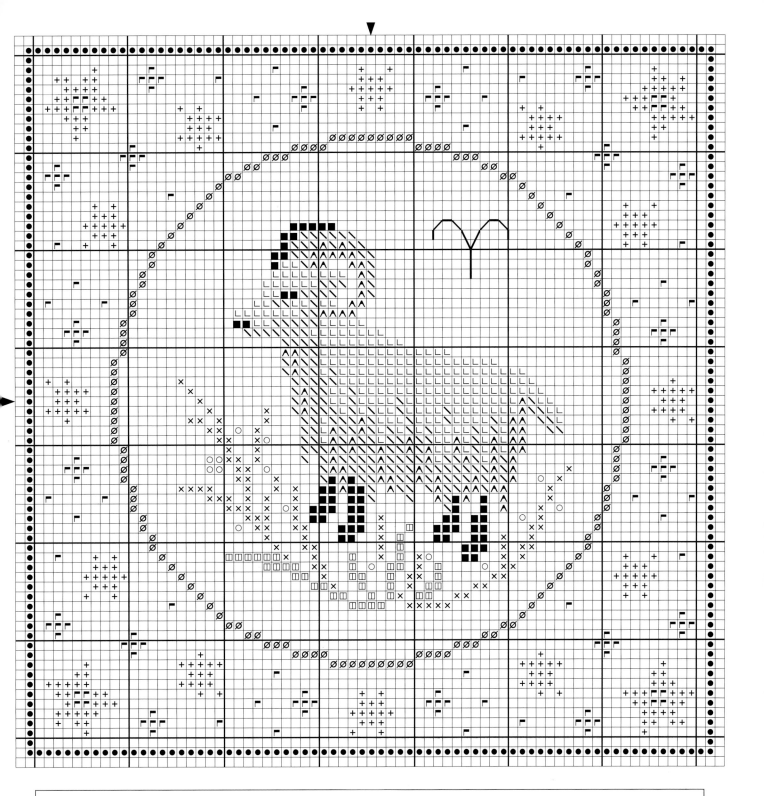

Symbol	Code	Color
⊞	703	dark green
⊠	907	light green
●	517	dark blue
⊘	807	light blue
■	844	darkest grey
◣	646	dark grey
◥	647	medium grey
⌐	3024	light grey
○	899	rose
⌐	972 + gold metallic thread, (1 strand of each)
+	444 + gold metallic thread, (1 strand of each)
—	646	dark grey (back stitch)

TAURUS

*T*aurus the bull is an earth sign represented by the planet Venus, the sapphire and the metal copper. This may give you ideas for personalizing the work.

Material
Linen with 10 threads per cm (25 threads per in)

Cutting size
22 x 22cm (8½ x 8½in)

Finished size
15 x 15cm (6 x 6in)

Thread
DMC embroidery thread or metallic thread. Use 2 strands in the needle

Finishing
See page 19 for instructions on making rectangular table linen

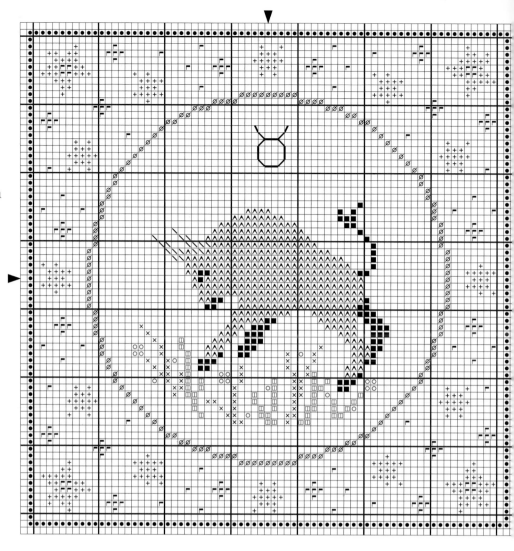

⊞	703	dark green
⊠	907	light green
●	517	dark blue
∅	807	light blue
■	310	black
▲	844	dark grey
◥	3022	light grey
⊙	899	rose
⌐	972 +	gold metallic thread, (1 strand of each)
⊞	444 +	gold metallic thread, (1 strand of each)
—	3022	light grey (back stitch)

GEMINI

An air sign known for its mutable nature, the twins are linked both with the planet and the metal Mercury. The mottled tiger's eye is its gemstone.

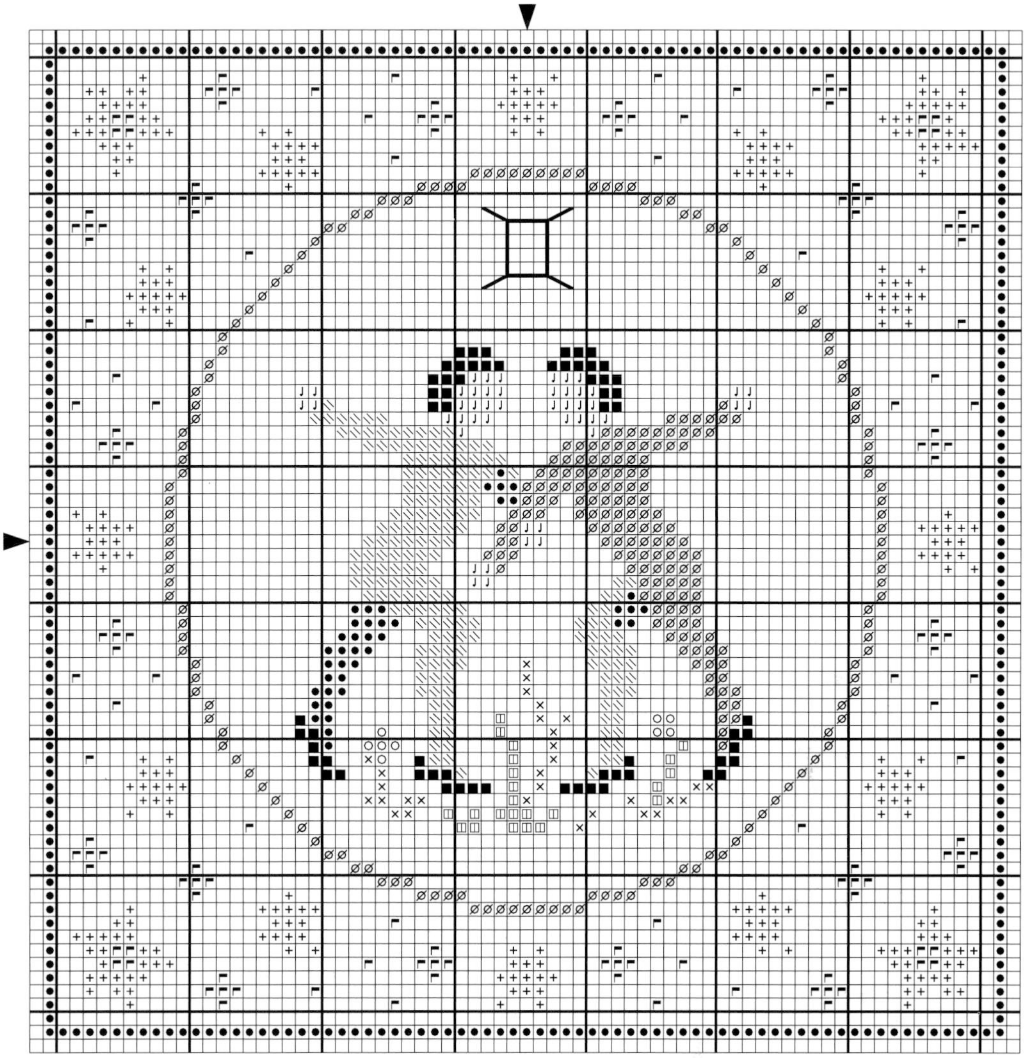

Material
Linen with 10 threads per cm (25 threads per in)

Cutting size
22 x 22cm ($8\frac{1}{2}$ x $8\frac{1}{2}$in)

Finished size
15 x 15cm (6 x 6in)

Thread
DMC embroidery thread or metallic thread. Use 2 strands in the needle

Finishing
See page 19 on making rectangular table linen

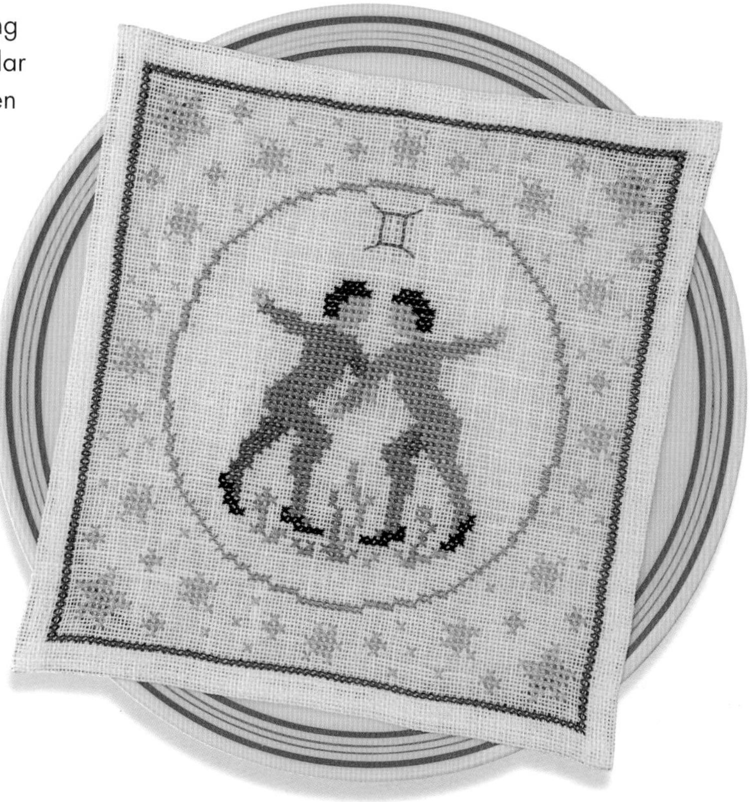

Symbol	No.	Colour
◫	703	dark green
☒	907	light green
●	517	dark blue
⧅	806	medium blue
ø	807	light blue
○	899	rose
■	310	black
♩	224	flesh
▀	972	+ gold metallic thread, (1 strand of each)
+	444	+ gold metallic thread, (1 strand of each)
—	3022	grey (back stitch)

CANCER

*B*lues and greens are appropriate for this water sign, or you may like to embroider Moons with white and silver metallic thread instead of the stars for this lunar-influenced star sign.

Material
Linen with 10 threads per cm (25 threads per in)

Cutting size
22 x 22cm (8½ x 8½in)

Finished size
15 x 15cm (6 x 6in)

Thread
DMC embroidery thread or metallic thread. Use 2 strands in the needle

Finishing
See page 19 for instructions on making rectangular table linen

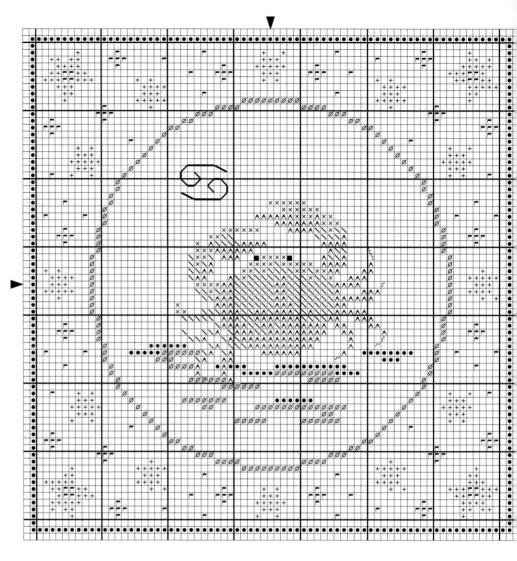

⊙	517	dark blue
⊘	807	light blue
■	310	black
▲	433	brown
◥	301	rust
⊠	435	light brown
⌐	972	+ gold metallic thread, (1 strand of each)
+	444	+ gold metallic thread, (1 strand of each)
—	3022	grey (back stitch)
〜	433	brown (back stitch)

LEO

*T*ry a ruby red or gold border for this fire sign, most strongly influenced by the Sun.

Material
Linen with 10 threads per cm (25 threads per in)

Cutting size
22 x 22cm (8½ x 8½in)

Finished size
15 x 15cm (6 x 6in)

Thread
DMC embroidery thread or metallic thread. Use 2 strands in the needle

Finishing
See page 19 for instructions on making rectangular table linen

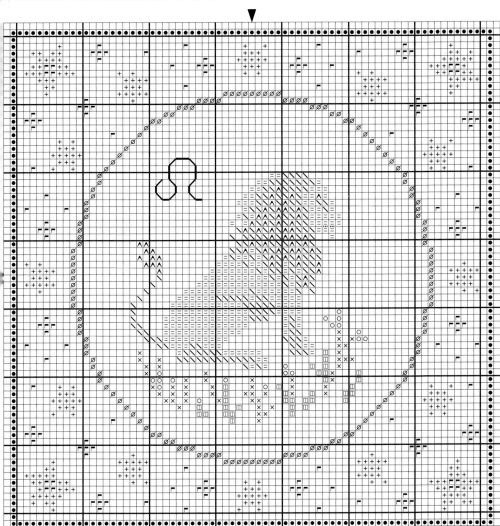

●	517	dark blue
Ø	807	light blue
∧	869	brown
◣	680	dark golden
⊟	729	light golden
⊙	553	lilac
⊞	703	dark green
⊠	907	light green
⌐	972	+ gold metallic thread, (1 strand of each)
⊞	444	+ gold metallic thread, (1 strand of each)
—	3022	grey (back stitch)
......	869	brown (back stitch)

VIRGO

*R*ed-brown and white
are the colours of the
sardonyx, the earth sign
Virgo's stone. It is also
influenced by the planet
Mercury.

Material

Linen with 10 threads per cm
(25 threads per in)

Cutting size

22 x 22cm (8½ x 8½in)

Finished size

15 x 15cm (6 x 6in)

Thread

DMC embroidery thread or
metallic thread. Use 2
strands in the needle

Finishing

See page 19
for instructions
on making
rectangular
table linen

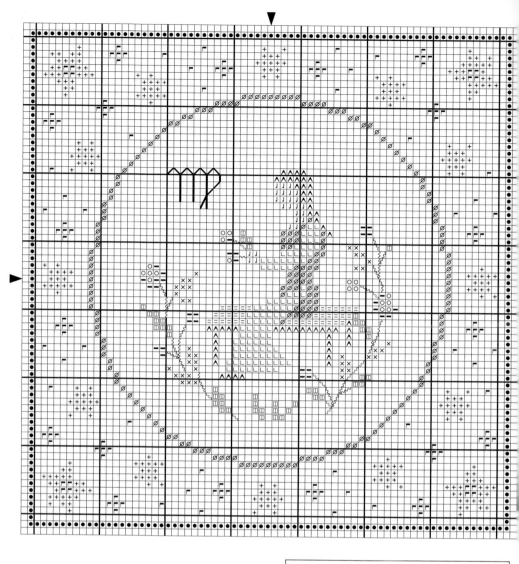

●	517	dark blue
⊘	807	light blue
L	598	light turquoise
⊟	3731	dark rose
⊙	899	light rose
J	224	flesh
▲	869	brown
⊟	729	golden
⊞	703	dark green
✕	907	light green
⊡	972	+ gold metallic thread, (1 strand of each)
+	444	+ gold metallic thread, (1 strand of each)
—	3022	grey (back stitch)
∿	703	dark green (back stitch)

LIBRA

The air sign of the scales relates to the planet Venus and the beautiful blue of the sapphire.

Material

Linen with 10 threads per cm (25 threads per in)

Cutting size

22 x 22cm (8½ x 8½in)

Finished size

15 x 15cm (6 x 6in)

Thread

DMC embroidery thread or metallic thread. Use 2 strands in the needle

Finishing

See page 19 for instructions on making rectangular table linen

●	517	dark blue
∅	807	light blue
◮	680	golden
⊟	729	light golden
◑	987	dark green
⊠	703	light green
◲	3731	dark rose
◎	899	light rose
⌐	972	+ gold metallic thread, (1 strand of each)
⊞	444	+ gold metallic thread, (1 strand of each)
—	3022	grey (back stitch)
∞∞∞	987	dark green (back stitch)

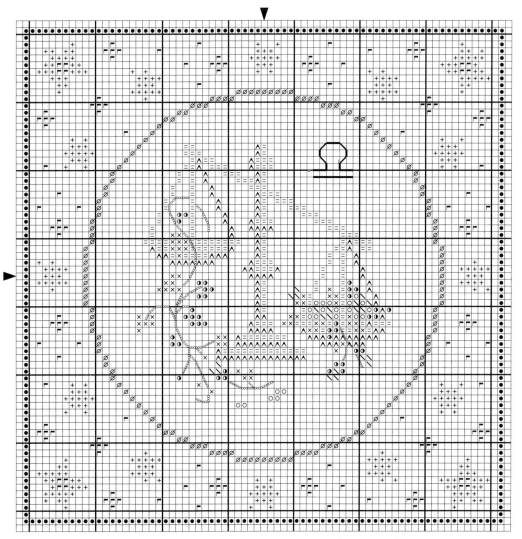

SCORPIO

*T*he second water sign claims the yellow or green jasper stone and the planet Pluto as its representatives.

Material
Linen with 10 threads per cm (25 threads per in)

Cutting size
22 x 22cm (8½ x 8½in)

Finished size
15 x 15cm (6 x 6in)

Thread
DMC embroidery thread or metallic thread. Use 2 strands in the needle

Finishing
See page 19 for instructions on making rectangular table linen

●	517	dark blue
⊘	807	light blue
◣	3781	dark brown
▲	869	medium brown
⊟	680	light brown
⊙	553	lilac
⊞	703	green
⊠	907	light green
⌐	972	+ gold metallic thread, (1 strand of each)
⊞	444	+ gold metallic thread, (1 strand of each)
▪	3022	grey
—	3022	grey (back stitch)
·····	3781	dark brown (back stitch)

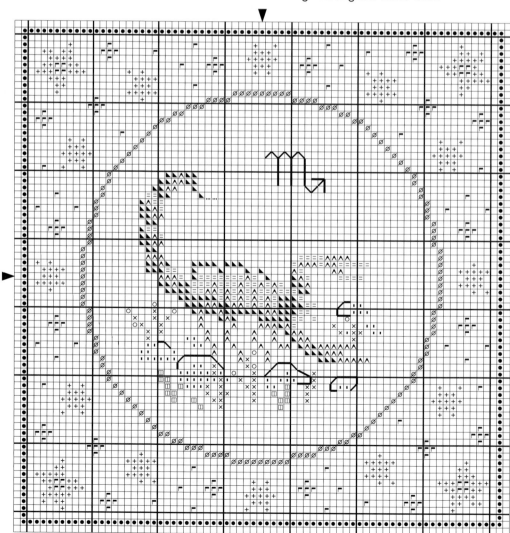

SAGITTARIUS

*J*upiter is the planet which relates to the archer, along with the topaz. The arrow symbol could also be used as a border motif.

Material
Linen with 10 threads per cm (25 threads per in)

Cutting size
22 x 22cm (8½ x 8½in)

Finished size
15 x 15cm (6 x 6in)

Thread
DMC embroidery thread or metallic thread. Use 2 strands in the needle

Finishing
See page 19 for instructions on making rectangular table linen

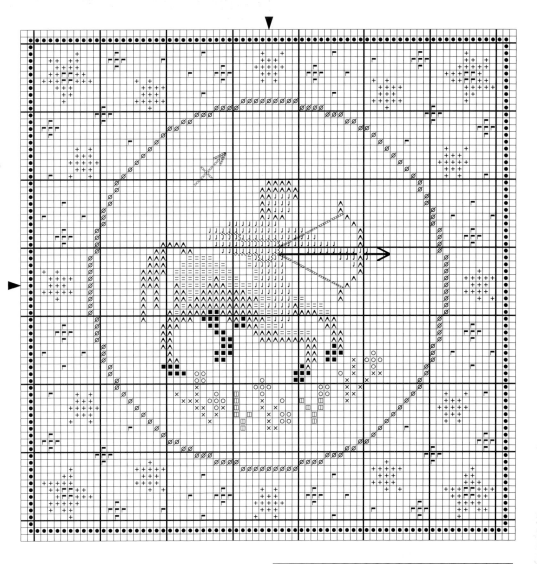

●	517 dark blue
⊘	807 light blue
⊞	703 dark green
✕	907 light green
■	3781 dark brown
◮	869 medium brown
⊟	680 light brown
◯	3731 rose
⏌	224 flesh
⌐	972 + gold metallic thread, (1 strand of each)
⊞	444 + gold metallic thread, (1 strand of each)
∞∞∞∞	3022 grey (back stitch)
—	869 medium brown (back stitch)
⌁⌁⌁	680 light brown (back stitch)

CAPRICORN

*T*he distinctive shape of Saturn would make an excellent border motif for Capricon. Its gemstone is the black onyx.

Material
Linen with 10 threads per cm (25 threads per in)

Cutting size
22 x 22cm (8½ x 8½in)

Finished size
15 x 15cm (6 x 6in)

Thread
DMC embroidery thread or metallic thread. Use 2 strands in the needle

Finishing
See page 19 for instructions on making rectangular table linen

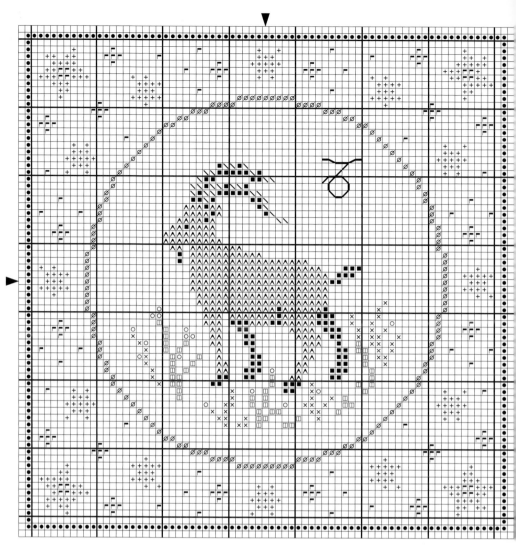

●	517	dark blue
⊘	807	light blue
⊡	703	dark green
⊠	907	light green
■	3781	dark brown
▲	869	light brown
⊙	553	lilac
◣	3022	grey
▣	972	+ gold metallic thread, (1 strand of each)
⊞	444	+ gold metallic thread, (1 strand of each)
—	3022	grey (back stitch)

AQUARIUS

Cool blues and greens would complement this water sign, or the lilacs and purples of the amethyst.

Material
Linen with 10 threads per cm (25 threads per in)

Cutting size
22 x 22cm (8½ x 8½in)

Finished size
15 x 15cm (6 x 6in)

Thread
DMC embroidery thread or metallic thread. Use 2 strands in the needle

Finishing
See page 19 for instructions on making rectangular table linen

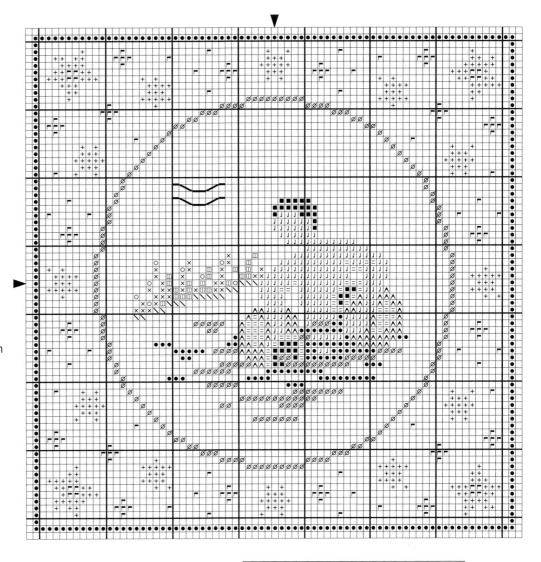

●	517	dark blue
Ø	807	light blue
⊞	703	dark green
✕	907	light green
■	3781	dark brown
◥	3022	grey
J	224	flesh
▲	920	dark rust
=	922	light rust
O	972	yellow
⌐	972	+ gold metallic thread, (1 strand of each)
+	444	+ gold metallic thread, (1 strand of each)
—	3022	grey (back stitch)

PISCES

*T*he final sign of the zodiac is another water sign, associated with Neptune and the moonstone, so silvery blue colours would be a good choice. ▶

Material
Linen with 10 threads per cm (25 threads per in)

Cutting size
22 x 22cm (8½ x 8½in)

Finished size
15 x 15cm (6 x 6in)

Thread
DMC embroidery thread or metallic thread. Use 2 strands in the needle

Finishing
See page 19 for instructions on making rectangular table linen

■	930	darkest blue
●	517	dark blue
⊘	807	light blue
◩	598	lightest blue
▲	922	rust
⊞	703	dark green
⊠	907	light green
⌐	972	+ gold metallic thread, (1 strand of each)
⊞	444	+ gold metallic thread, (1 strand of each)
—	3022	grey (back stitch)

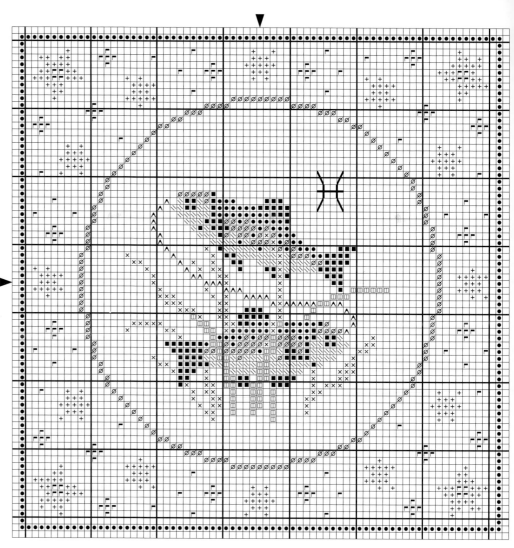

CHRISTMAS GARLAND JAR COVER

*D*on't just think jar covers have to be for preserves. Use them to add that personal touch to a gift of toiletries or cosmetics. Include a small initial in the heart for a personal gift.

Materials

Linen with 10 threads per cm
  (25 threads per in)
50cm (20in) bias binding
80cm (31in) ribbon

Cutting size

16 x 16cm (6½ x 6½in)

Finished size

15cm (6in) diameter circle

Thread

DMC embroidery thread. Use 2
  strands in the needle

Finishing

See page 19 for instructions on
  making a jar cover

⊡	321	dark red
⊡	891	medium red
⊠	3706	light red
◇	444	yellow
✳	905	green
– –	905	green (back stitch)

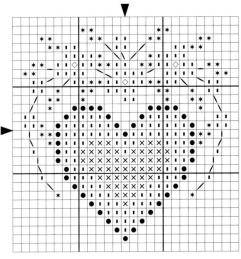

FESTIVE QUILTED PLACE MAT

Υour Christmas table will look wonderful with these bright place mats, or you can adapt the design to make a table runner or tray cloth. Use ready-made Aida strip if you prefer.

Materials
White Aida with 4½ stitches per cm (11 stitches per in)
2 pieces 40 x 50cm (16 x 20in) checked cotton
40 x 50cm (16 x 20in) interfacing
2m (2yds) broad bias binding

Cutting size
White Aida 55 x 9cm (21½ x 3½in)

Finished size
38 x 48cm (15 x 19in)

Thread
DMC embroider thread. Use 3 strands in the needle

Finishing
See page 19 for instructions on making a place mat

▼	986	dark green
⊡	988	medium green
L	471	light green
◪	347	dark red
+	891	red
◇	444	yellow
--	310	black (back stitch)

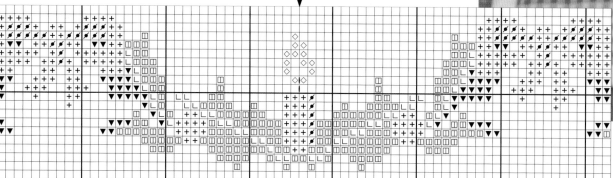

CHRISTMAS CLOTH

*U*se this design to make a small cloth for a coffee table, or extend the border to fit a larger cloth. Work the design from the corner, then turn the chart 90 degrees and continue with the second corner, and so on.

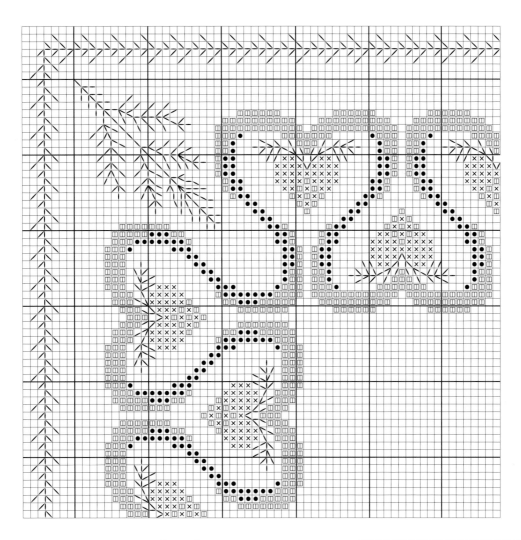

Material

White Aida with 4½ stitches
  per cm (11 stitches per in)

Cutting size

40 x 40cm (16 x 16in)

Finished size

37 x 37 cm (14¾ x 14¾in)

Thread

DMC embroidery thread. Use 3
strand in the needle
Metallic thread. Use 1 strand in
the needle

Finishing

See page 19 for instructions on
making a rectangular cloth

●	498	dark red
⊞	606	bright red
☒		gold metallic thread
--	905	dark green (back stitch)

CHRISTMAS TABLE RUNNER

$\mathcal{C}$ount your stitches before you start so that you position the design correctly on the fabric. Start at the top left-hand corner and continue to repeat the design across the top of the fabric, then turn and continue round the edge.

Material
White Aida with 4½ stitches per cm (11 stitches per in)

Cutting size
30 x 46cm (12 x 18in)

Finished size
24 x 41cm (9½ x 16½in)

Thread
DMC embroidery thread. Use 2 strands in the needle
Metallic thread. Use 1 strand in the needle

Finishing
See page 17 for instructions on making a table runner

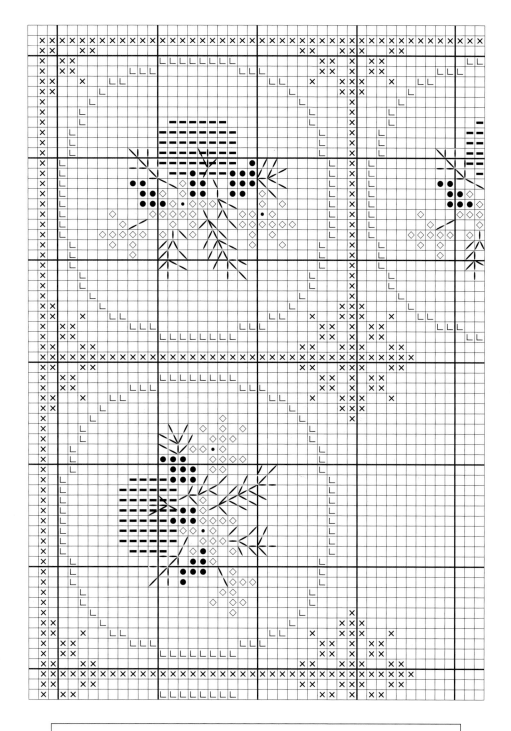

■	831 brown	◇	891 red
●	904 dark green	⊠	gold metallic thread
L	472 light green	--	906 medium green
•	444 yellow		(back stitch)

POINSETTIA BORDER

$\mathcal{T}$he vibrant colours of the Mexican poinsettia, *Euphorbia pulcherrima*, make a colourful border to decorate a mantelpiece, table or lamp. You can embroider on ready-made border strips of evenweave fabric.

Material
Linen with 10 threads per cm
(25 threads per in)

Cutting size
10cm (4in) deep

Finished size
10cm (4in) deep

Thread
DMC embroidery thread.
Use 2 strands in the needle
Metallic thread. Use 1 strand
in the needle

Finishing
Hem the top and side edges
and finish the bottom of the
border with bias binding

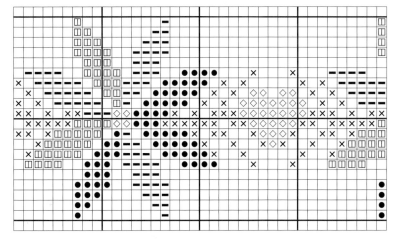

●	321	dark red
▬	891	medium red
▥	3706	light red
⊠	905	green
◇		gold metallic thread

7

BORDER AND
MOTIF PROJECTS

This final chapter contains a series of wonderful projects for your home. They combine the use of borders and motifs to give small, simple designs for jar covers or plate liners to more complex and demanding items like chair covers and tablecloths. Remember that you can always use projects as they are provided, but as soon as you find your confidence and your skills begin to grow, it will be most satisfying to be a little more imaginative and think about adapting existing designs and creating your own individual work.

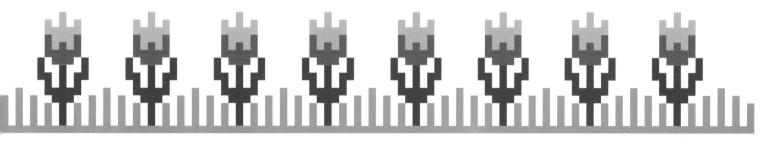

ORANGE JAR COVER

*S*mall circular motifs are useful for all sorts of projects from jar covers to the corner of handkerchiefs, or as a motif on the front of a recipe or notebook. The orange could make the basis of an all-over design.

Materials
Linen with 10 threads per cm
(25 threads per in)
60cm (24in) lace edging

Cutting size
16 x 16cm (6½ x 6½in)

Finished size
14cm (5½in) diameter
circle plus lace

Thread
DMC embroidery thread.
Use 2 strands in the needle

Finishing
See page 19 for instructions
on making a jar cover

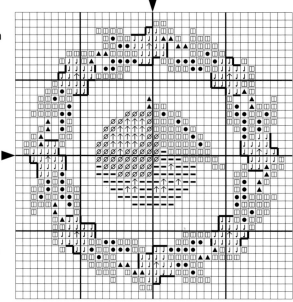

●	3346	dark green
⊞	906	light green
▲	869	brown
⊟	971	dark orange
⊘	741	medium orange
↑	972	light orange
J		white
—	524	light grey (back stitch)

APPLE JAR COVER

*I*f you are using a wide lace edging for a circular piece, ease the lace on to the fabric as you sew so that it lays flat at the outside edge. Alternatively, finish the edge with bias binding.

Materials
Linen with 10 threads per cm
  (25 threads per in)
60cm (24in) lace edging

Cutting size
16 x 16cm (6½ x 6½ in)

Finished size
14cm (5½in) diameter circle
  plus lace

Thread
DMC embroidery thread.
  Use 2 strands in the needle

Finishing
See page 19 for instructions
  on making a jar cover

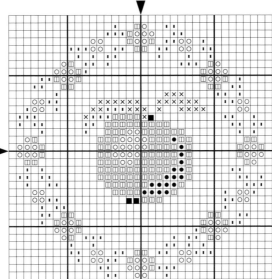

▣	469	dark green
⊠	581	light green
●	347	dark red
▥	350	red
◯	721	orange
■	3781	brown

CHERRY JAR COVER

*P*erfect for your home-made cherry jam, use an appropriate fruit motif depending
on the contents of the jar. You could create a break in the border to embroider
the words 'Cherry Jam'.

Materials
Linen with 10 threads per cm
(25 threads per in)
60cm (24in) lace edging

Cutting size
16 x 16cm (6½ x 6½ in)

Finished size
14cm (5½in) diameter
circle plus lace

Thread
DMC embroidery thread.
Use 2 strands in the needle

Finishing
See page 19 for instructions
on making a jar cover

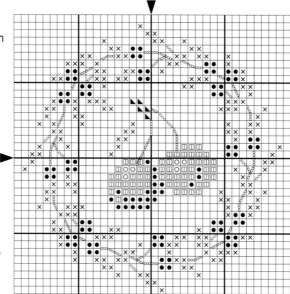

◣	831	brown
✕	581	green
●	347	dark red
ⅠⅠ	350	red
◎	950	rose
∘∘∘∘∘∘	831	brown (back stitch)

☒ 3362 dark green

FLOWER AND BUTTERFLY CUSHION

*T*his project uses a delightful combination of two motifs with an attractive, complementary border. Using a border means that you can utilize smaller embroidery panels as cushions.

Materials

White Aida with 4½ stitches per cm (11 stitches per in)
1m (1yd) x 120cm (48in) yellow fabric

Cutting size

25 x 30cm (10 x 12 in)

Finished size

31 x 49cm (12½ x 19½in)

Thread

DMC embroidery thread. Use 3 strands in the needle

Finishing

From the yellow fabric, cut a 43 x 38cm (17 x 15in) rectangle for the back and four strips 8cm (3¼in) wide for the front border. Sew the strips around the edge of the embroidery, making seams at 45 degrees from each corner, then trim to a rectangle. Continue following the instructions on page 18 for making a cushion

●	469	green
⊠	988	light green
◼	632	brown
▫	783	golden
⊠	725	yellow
◸	720	red
--	469	green (back stitch)
⧫⧫⧫⧫	632	brown (back stitch)

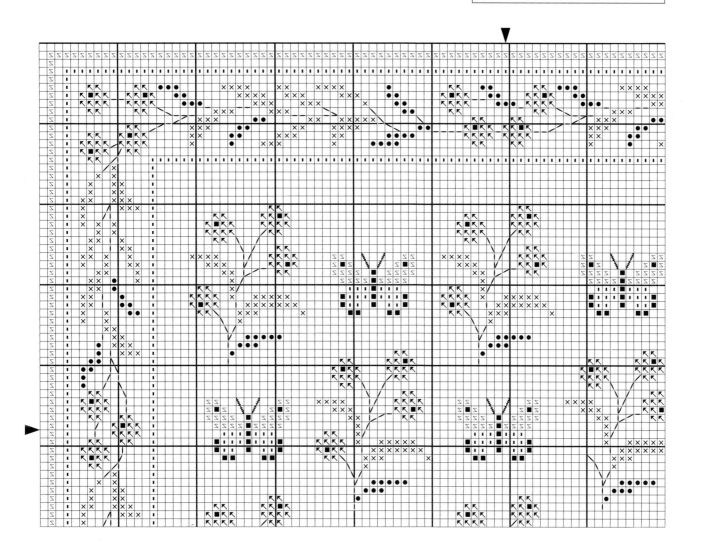

BLUEBELL CUSHION

*T*his charming all-over design shows how a simple motif can be repeated to create a dramatic pattern. All-over designs can use one single motif or a collection of related motifs.

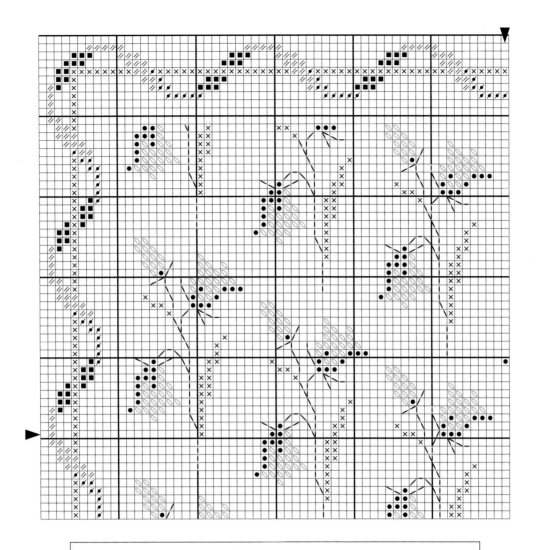

■	400 dark rust		●	3807 blue
◪	976 medium rust		◩	799 light blue
◨	402 light rust		––	904 dark green
✕	988 light green			

Materials

White Aida with 4½ stitches
per cm (11 stitches per in)
1m (1yd) x 120cm (48in) blue
fabric

Cutting size

25 x 30cm (10 x 12 in)

Finished size

31 x 40cm (12½ x 16in)

Thread

DMC embroidery thread. Use 3
strands in the needle

Finishing

From the blue fabric, cut a
31 x 40cm (12½ x 16in)
rectangle for the back and four

strips 8cm (3¼in) wide for the
front border. Sew the strips
around the edge of the
embroidery, extending the seams
beyond one end of the
embroidery in each case, then
trim to a rectangle. Continue
following the instructions on page
18 for making a cushion

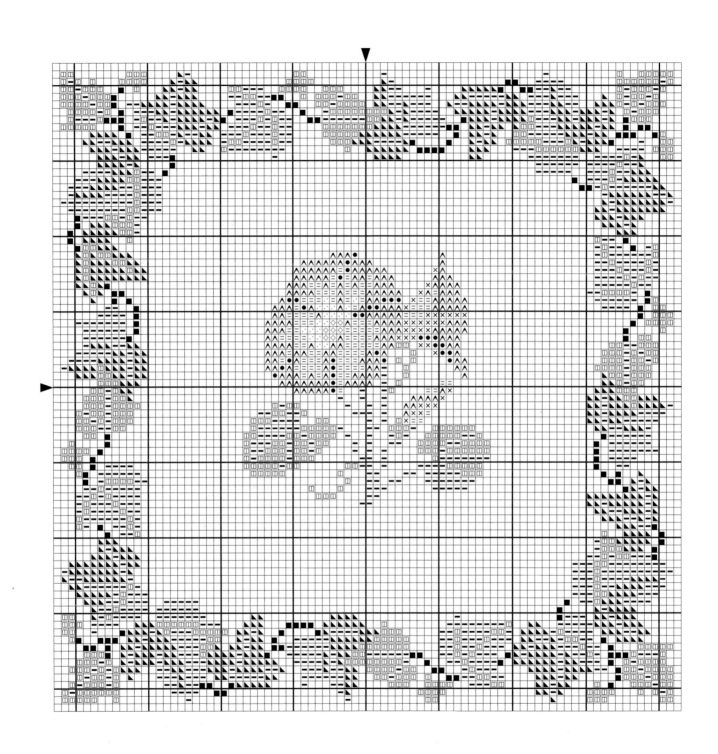

CONVOLVULUS CUSHION

Enlarging a fairly small flower gives you the chance to concentrate on the detail of shaping and colour in the bloom.

■	830	brown
◣	986	dark green
▬	905	medium green
▥	704	light green
☒	472	lightest green
⊡		white
⧇	973	yellow
●	333	dark blue
▲	340	medium blue
▤	341	light blue

Materials
Linen with 8 thread per cm (20 threads per in)
1m (1yd) x 120cm (48in) wide blue checked fabric

Cutting size
Linen 28 x 28cm (11 x 11in)

Finished size
46 x 46cm (18 x 18in)

Thread
DMC embroidery thread. Use 3 strands in the needle

Finishing
From the check fabric, cut a 46 x 46cm (18 x 18in) square for the back and four strips 12cm (4½in) wide for the front border. Sew the strips around the edge of the embroidery, making seams at 45 degrees for each corner. and trim to a rectangle. Continue following the instructions on page 18 for making a cushion, running a row of machine stitching 2cm (³⁄₄in) from the outside edge of the cushion

ANEMONE SPRAY PLACE MAT

$\mathcal{A}$s with all border designs, make sure you count your work carefully before you start. Work the first corner, then turn the chart 90 degrees and work the next corner in the same way. This delightful motif features *Anemone hepatica*.

Materials
Linen with 10 threads per cm
  (25 threads per in)
80cm (31in) lace edging

Cutting size
40 x 48cm (16 x 19in)

Finished size
35 x 43cm (14 x 17in)

Thread
DMC embroidery thread. Use
  2 strands in the needle

Finishing
See page 19 for instructions
  on making a place mat

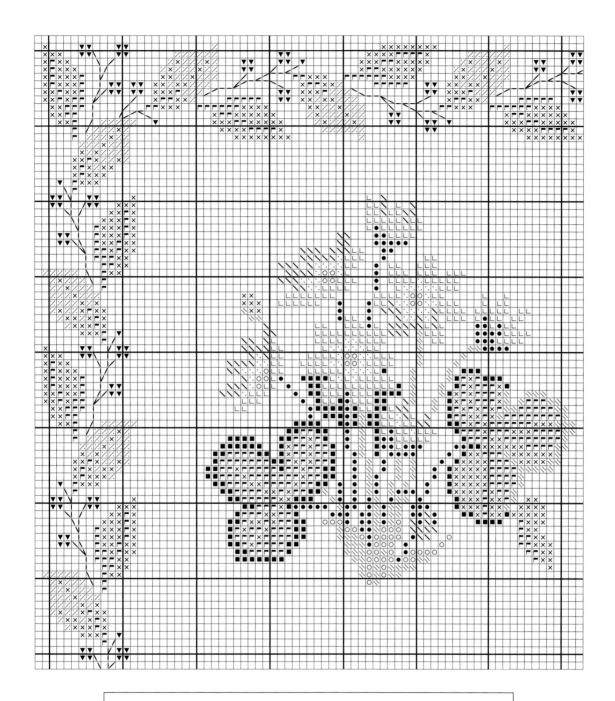

	580 dark green			white
	470 medium green			333 blue
	471 light green			340 light blue
	829 brown			221 dark red
	831 light brown	-- --		470 medium green (back stitch)
	734 light yellow-green			
	407 red-beige			

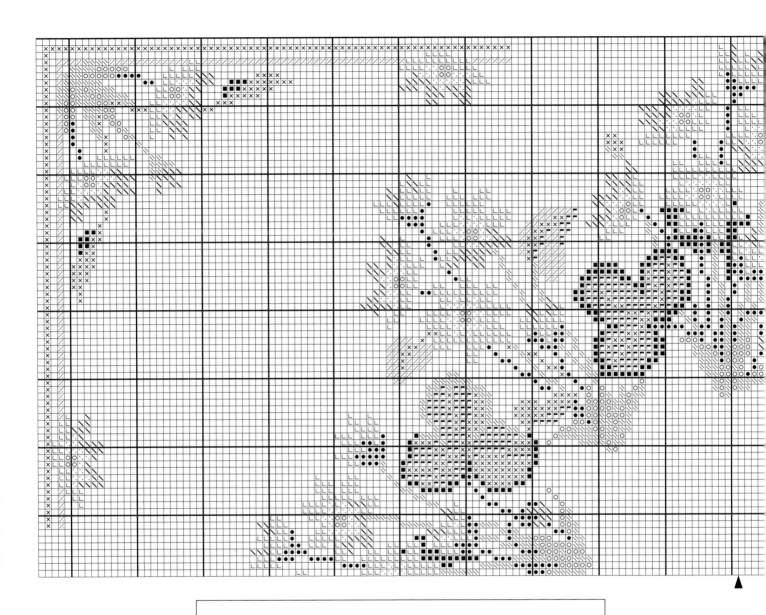

▣	580	dark green	◎	734	light yellow-green
☒	470	medium green	⬤	407	red-beige
▨	3348	light green	⋅		white
◼	829	brown	◥	333	blue
◩	831	light brown	◱	340	light blue

ANEMONE CLOTH

*A*lso using *Anemone hepatica*, you could feature the central motif on a circular cloth, or link the border with an all-over central design. Stitch one-quarter of the design from the chart, then turn it 90 degrees and continue to stitch.

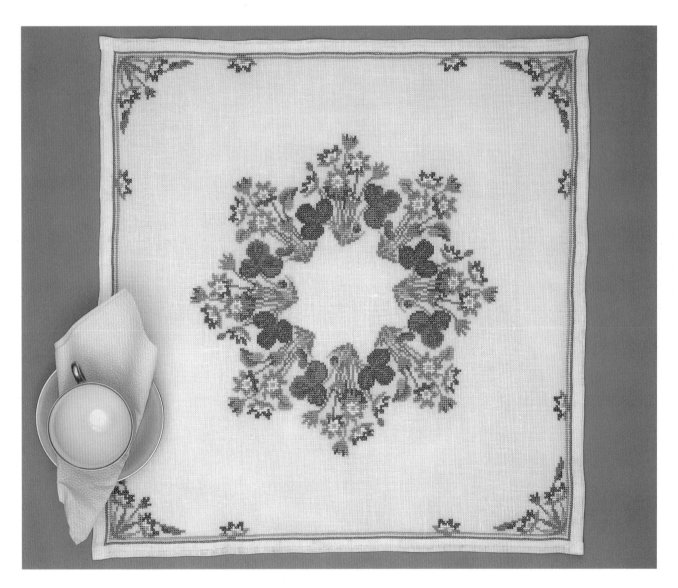

Material
Linen with 10 threads per cm (25 threads per in)

Cutting size
50 x 50cm (20 x 20in)

Finished size
46 x 46cm (18 x 18in)

Thread
DMC embroidery thread. Use 2 strands in the needle

Finishing
See page 19 for instructions on making a table cloth

YELLOW ARCHANGEL WITH BUTTERFLIES

A charming project for the more experienced cross stitcher, this wonderful wall hanging featuring *Lamiastrum galeobdolon* would make an attractive addition to any home.

Material
Linen with 8 threads per cm (20 threads per in)

Cutting size
41 x 35cm ($17\frac{1}{2}$ x 14in)

Finished size
36 x 30cm ($14\frac{1}{4}$ x 12in)

Thread
DMC embroidery thread. Use 3 strands in the needle

Finishing
See page 17 for instructions on making a wall hanging

Border

▀	611	beige
Ø	372	light beige
S	741	orange
=	444	yellow
J	307	light yellow
∩	906	bright green
—	3346	dark green (back stitch)
○○○○○	611	beige (back stitch)

Motif

◣	3346	dark green
▬	470	medium green
╲	471	light green
//	732	dull green
■	3371	dark brown
◢	3781	medium brown
H	433	yellow-brown
×	976	copper
◇	971	orange
‖‖‖	977	light copper
+	3821	yellow
▲	797	blue
◫	793	light blue
⧅	318	grey
⊢	3072	light grey
••••••	3371	dark brown (back stitch)
~~	3781	medium brown (back stitch)

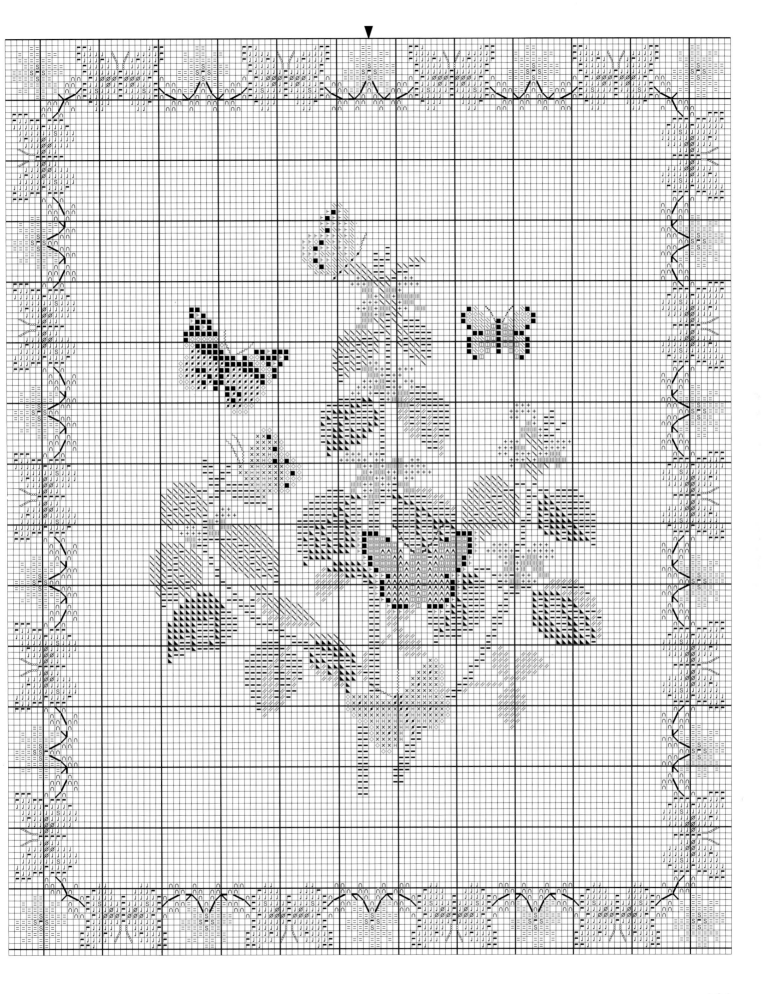

BLUEBELL AND RIBBON PANEL

*U*sing a ribbon-effect embroidery to separate repeated motifs is an interesting
way to create an all-over design.

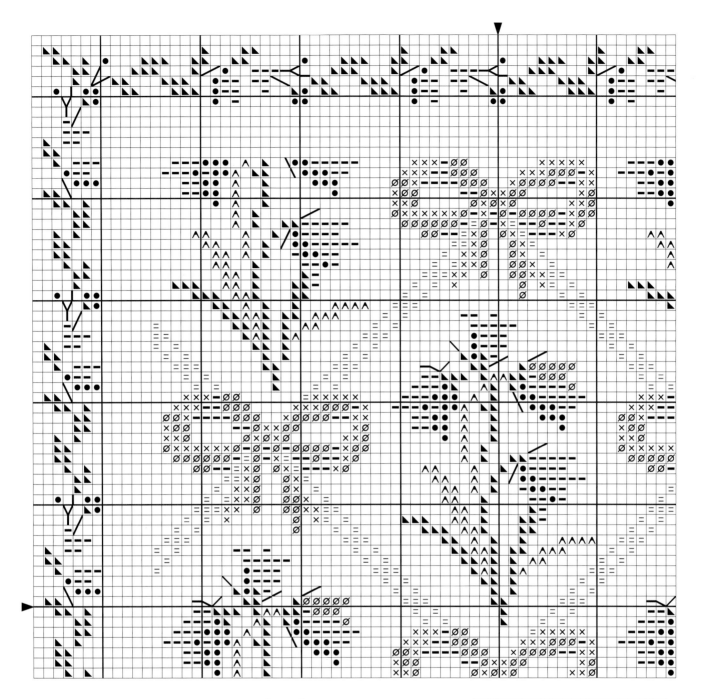

Material
Linen with 8 threads per cm
(20 threads per in)

Cutting size
35 x 30cm (14 x 12in)

Finished size
30 x 25cm (12 x 10in)

Thread
DMC embroidery thread. Use 3
strands in the needle

Finishing
See page 17 for instructions on
making a wall hanging

◣	987	dark green
◭	368	light green
⊙	333	dark blue
⊟	340	medium blue
⊘	341	light blue
⊠	775	lightest blue
⊟	372	beige
—	987	dark green (back stitch)

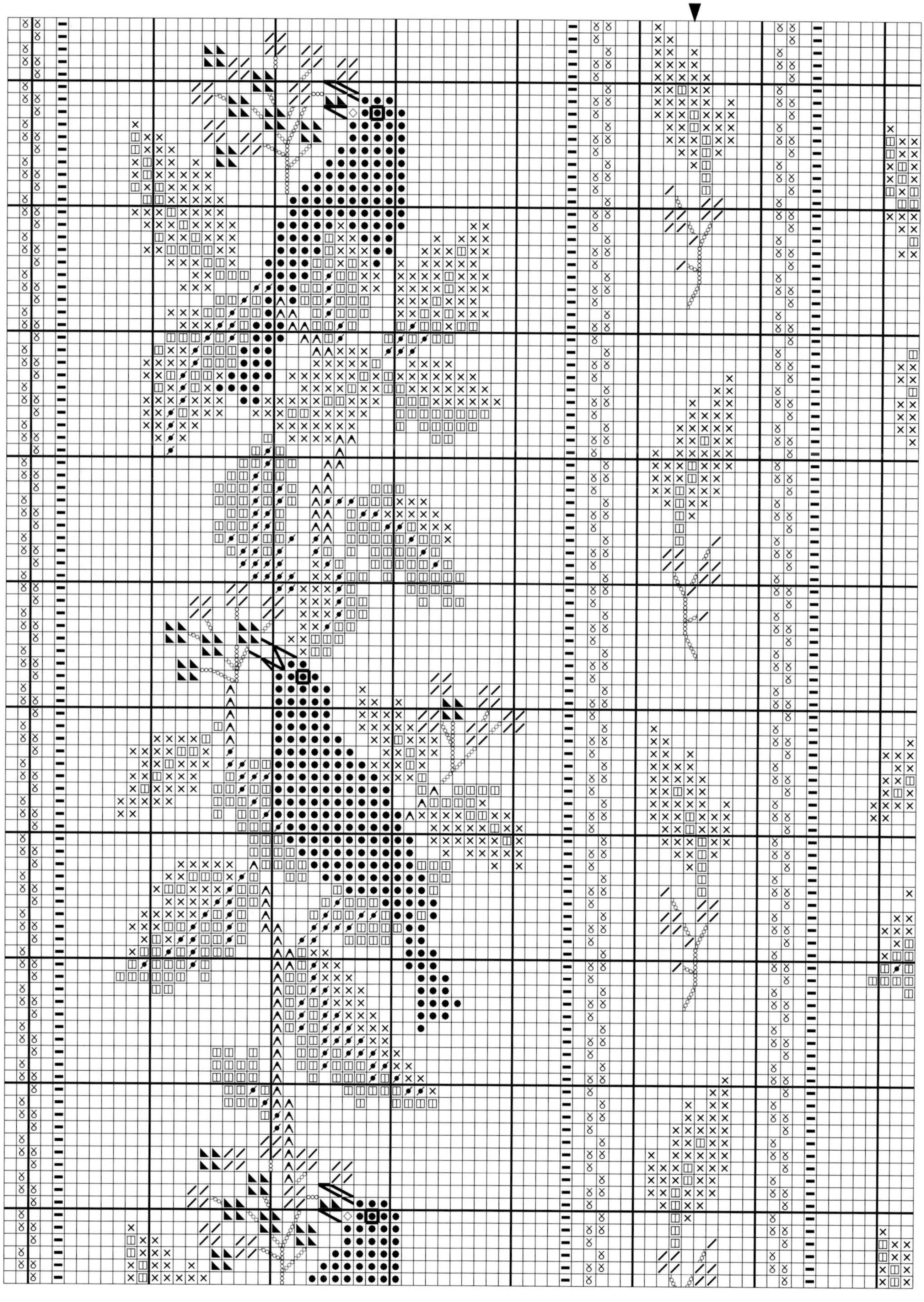

SEAT COVER WITH BLACKBIRDS

*U*sing canvas and tapestry wool would be a good idea for a more hard-wearing seat cover.

Material
Beige Aida with 5 stitches per cm
(13 stitches per in)

Cutting size
To find the correct size, place a
sheet of greaseproof (waxed) paper
over your chair seat and draw the
outline of it, leaving 2cm (³/₄in)
extra for seam and shrinkage
allowance. Place the pattern on the
fabric and tack (baste) along the
outline. Find the centre of the fabric
and the chart and begin stitching
from there, covering all the material

Thread
DMC embroidery thread. Use 3
strands in the needle

Symbol	Code	Colour
●	310	black
▬	610	brown
8	435	bronze
▲	731	dull green
◪	987	dark green
▥	470	medium green
☒	3348	light green
◣	347	dark red
☑	946	bright red
◈	741	orange
∞∞∞∞	731	dull green (back stitch)
—	741	orange (back stitch)

Finishing
Press the finished embroidery
lightly. Lift out the chair seat the
attach the embroidery with
upholstery tacks. Replace the
chair seat. If you are making a
separate chair cushion, see page
18 for instructions on making a
cushion, but fill with a piece of
foam rather than stuffing

FOOTSTOOL

This project shows how you can combine two border designs to create a pleasing pattern. For a more hard-wearing footstool, you could use canvas and tapestry wool.

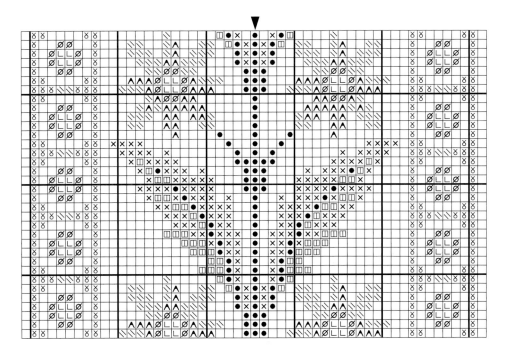

	580 dull green
	905 dark green
	907 light green
	976 bronze
	972 dark yellow
	444 light yellow
	799 blue
	341 light blue

Material
White Aida with 5 stitches per cm (13 stitches per in)

Cutting size
To find the correct size, place a sheet of greaseproof (waxed) paper over your footstool and draw the outline of it, leaving 2cm (³⁄₄in) extra for seam and shrinkage allowance. Place the pattern on the fabric and tack (baste) along the outline. Find the centre of the fabric and the chart and begin stitching from there, covering all the material

Thread
DMC embroidery thread. Use 3 strands in the needle

Finishing
Press the finished embroidery lightly. Place it on the footstool and fasten it with upholstery tacks. Cover the edges with braid and fasten with more tacks or with upholstery glue

INDEX